Through the Pulse

The Story of Kompany

Mei Raj

ISBN: 9781779693921
Imprint: Telephasic Workshop
Copyright © 2024 Mei Raj.
All Rights Reserved.

Contents

Introduction	**1**
The Formation of Kompany	1
Chapter One: A Journey Begins	**9**
The Early Days	9
Rise to Local Fame	14
Bibliography	**19**
Bibliography	**25**
The Road to the First Album	25
Chapter Highlights:	33
Chapter Two: The Spotlight Shines Brighter	**41**
National Success	41
Headlining Tours and Sold-Out Shows	47
Behind the Scenes	53
Chapter Highlights:	59
Chapter Three: Trials and Triumphs	**67**
Internal Struggles	67
Bibliography	**75**
The Breakup Rumors	75
Rebirth and Reinvention	82
Bibliography	**91**
Chapter Highlights:	91

Chapter Four: Legacy and Impact   **99**
Influencing a New Generation   99
Philanthropy and Activism   105
Kompany's Cultural Impact   112
Chapter Highlights: 118

Conclusion   **125**
Kompany: Forever in the Hearts of Fans   125

Acknowledgements   **133**
Thanking the fans and supporters   133
Recognizing the contributions of the band members   133
Appreciation for the team behind Kompany's success   133

Appendix   **135**
Discography   135
Timeline of Significant Events   143
Additional Interviews and Quotes   148
Kompany's Top Ten Songs   152
Resources and Recommended Reading   157
About the Author   160

Index   **167**

Introduction

The Formation of Kompany

Childhood friends with a shared passion for music

From the very beginning, the story of Kompany is one woven with the threads of friendship and shared dreams. Growing up in a small town, the members of Kompany—each a unique note in the symphony of life—discovered their passion for music at an early age. It was in the sun-drenched afternoons of their childhood that they first began to explore the sounds that would eventually define them.

The foundation of their bond was built on a mutual love for music, a love that transcended the ordinary. They would gather in basements and backyards, strumming guitars and beating on makeshift drums, creating melodies that echoed the innocence of their youth. The music they created was raw and unfiltered, a reflection of their unrefined skills but also of their unyielding enthusiasm. It was during these formative years that they began to understand the power of music as a means of expression, a way to articulate feelings that words often failed to capture.

$$E = mc^2 \tag{1}$$

While this famous equation by Einstein might not seem directly related to music, it serves as a metaphor for the energy that music creates. Just as mass can be converted into energy, so too can the raw emotions of childhood friendships be transformed into the powerful energy of musical expression. The synergy between the band members created a dynamic that was palpable; they were not just friends but collaborators in a shared creative journey.

As they navigated the trials of adolescence, their bond deepened. Music became a sanctuary, a refuge from the challenges of growing up. They faced typical teenage problems: the awkwardness of first crushes, the sting of rejection, and the pressure to fit in. Yet, through it all, they found solace in their shared passion. The act of creating music allowed them to process their experiences, turning their struggles into songs that resonated with their own lives and, eventually, with others.

Their early influences were diverse, ranging from classic rock legends to the emerging pop sounds of the time. Each member brought their own unique tastes to the mix, creating a rich tapestry of influences that would shape their sound. They spent countless hours listening to vinyl records, dissecting the intricacies of their favorite songs, and dreaming of one day being on the same stage as their idols. This eclectic mix of influences not only enriched their musical repertoire but also laid the groundwork for the innovative sound that Kompany would later become known for.

In these early days, they also faced their share of challenges. The dream of becoming musicians was often met with skepticism from those around them. Friends and family would question the viability of a career in music, urging them to pursue more traditional paths. Yet, the strength of their friendship and their shared passion for music acted as a shield against the doubts of the world. They were determined to carve out their own path, one that resonated with their true selves.

The journey was not without its bumps. There were disagreements over musical direction, moments of self-doubt, and the ever-looming fear of failure. However, these struggles only served to strengthen their bond. They learned to communicate openly, to compromise, and to support each other through thick and thin. This foundation of trust and collaboration would prove invaluable as they moved forward in their musical journey.

In essence, the early days of Kompany were marked by a profound connection—a connection that was not solely about music but about friendship, growth, and the pursuit of a shared dream. As they transitioned from childhood friends to aspiring musicians, they carried with them the lessons learned during those formative years. The spirit of collaboration and the unwavering passion for music became the driving forces behind their journey, propelling them toward the realization of their dreams.

As they took their first steps into the wider world of music, they did so with a sense of purpose and a deep-rooted belief in the power of their friendship. It was this bond that would carry them through the challenges ahead and inspire the creation of the music that would ultimately define Kompany.

Influences and early musical experiences

The journey of Kompany began not just with a shared passion for music but also through the rich tapestry of influences that shaped each member's artistic identity. Growing up in a world saturated with diverse musical genres, the band members were exposed to an array of sounds that would later inform their unique style. From pop to rock, jazz to folk, these early musical experiences provided a foundation that would prove invaluable as they navigated their path in the music industry.

Diverse Musical Backgrounds

The members of Kompany hailed from varied musical backgrounds, which contributed to a melting pot of influences. For instance, lead vocalist Alex, raised in a household where classic rock was the soundtrack of his youth, found inspiration in the powerful ballads of legends like *Freddie Mercury* and *Janis Joplin*. Their emotive delivery and lyrical depth resonated with him, igniting a desire to convey similar feelings through his own music.

Meanwhile, guitarist Sarah, influenced by her parents' eclectic vinyl collection, absorbed sounds from *The Beatles* to *Nina Simone*. This exposure to different genres fostered her appreciation for melody and harmony, leading her to experiment with various styles, ultimately shaping the band's signature sound.

Early Musical Experiences

The early musical experiences of Kompany members were pivotal in honing their craft. Each member participated in school bands, local choirs, and community theater productions, where they not only developed their musical abilities but also learned the importance of collaboration and teamwork. These formative experiences were crucial in establishing a sense of camaraderie among the band members, which would later translate into their on-stage chemistry.

For instance, during high school, drummer Jake formed a garage band with his friends. The group spent countless weekends jamming, covering songs from their favorite artists, and writing their own material. This period of experimentation was marked by both triumphs and failures, as they navigated the challenges of creating original music. One memorable experience involved a disastrous performance at a local talent show, where technical difficulties led to a cacophony of sound rather than the harmonious melodies they had envisioned. However, this setback taught them resilience and the importance of preparation, lessons that would serve them well in their future endeavors.

Influences from the Local Music Scene

Growing up in a vibrant local music scene also played a significant role in shaping Kompany's early influences. The band members frequently attended local gigs, where they were exposed to emerging artists and established acts alike. These experiences not only fueled their passion for music but also provided them with a sense of community and belonging.

One pivotal moment occurred when they attended a performance by a local indie band, *The Echoes*. The raw energy and authenticity of the band left a lasting impression on them, inspiring Kompany to embrace their individuality and pursue their own sound. The members of Kompany realized that music was not just about technical proficiency; it was about connecting with an audience and sharing genuine emotions.

Theoretical Framework of Musical Influence

To understand the influences that shaped Kompany, it is essential to consider the theoretical frameworks of musical influence. According to *Meyer's Theory of Musical Expectation*, listeners develop expectations based on their previous musical experiences. This concept suggests that the band members' early exposure to various genres and artists influenced their songwriting and performance styles.

The equation that represents this theory can be summarized as follows:

$$E = f(P, C) \qquad (2)$$

Where:

- E = Expectation
- P = Previous musical experiences
- C = Contextual influences (cultural, social, etc.)

In Kompany's case, their diverse backgrounds (P) combined with their local music scene experiences (C) created a rich reservoir of expectations that informed their musical output.

Challenges and Growth

Despite the myriad of influences, the path to finding their unique sound was not without challenges. The band faced moments of self-doubt and uncertainty, particularly during their early songwriting sessions. Each member grappled with the fear of not living up to the musical legends they admired, leading to creative blockages that hindered their progress.

To overcome these challenges, the band engaged in open dialogues about their artistic visions. They adopted a collaborative approach to songwriting, allowing each member to contribute their ideas and perspectives. This process not only strengthened their bond but also facilitated personal growth as they learned to embrace vulnerability and authenticity in their music.

Conclusion

In summary, the influences and early musical experiences that shaped Kompany were multifaceted and deeply intertwined. From diverse musical backgrounds and early performances to the vibrant local music scene, each element contributed to the band's identity. As they navigated the complexities of their artistic journey, these experiences laid the groundwork for the powerful connections they would forge with their audience, ultimately leading to the birth of Kompany—a dream come true that was just the beginning of a remarkable odyssey through the pulse of music.

The birth of Kompany - a dream come true

The story of Kompany begins not just as a band, but as a manifestation of youthful dreams and shared passions. Born from the hearts of childhood friends, the inception of Kompany was a moment that felt both inevitable and magical. As the boys gathered in their parents' basements, strumming on old guitars and banging on makeshift drums, they were not just making music; they were weaving the fabric of their future.

The Spark of Inspiration

In the early days, the spark of inspiration came from a myriad of sources. Each member brought their unique influences to the table, drawing from a rich tapestry of musical genres. From the soulful ballads of the past to the pulsating beats of contemporary pop, they found common ground in their eclectic tastes. This blend was not just an assortment of sounds; it became the foundation of their identity. The equation of their sound could be represented as:

$$S = f(G_1, G_2, G_3, \ldots, G_n) \tag{3}$$

where S is the sound of Kompany, and G_i represents the various genres that influenced their music.

Challenges Faced

However, the road to the birth of Kompany was not without its challenges. The boys faced the age-old problem of self-doubt, a hurdle that many aspiring musicians encounter. It was during one of their jam sessions that they realized the importance of perseverance. They began to understand that every great artist faced rejection and uncertainty. This realization was pivotal, as it solidified their commitment to their dream.

They often recalled the moment they decided to take their music public. It was a warm summer evening when they first performed at a local talent show. The nerves were palpable, yet the thrill of sharing their music with an audience was intoxicating. The applause that followed was not just validation; it was a sign that they were on the right path.

The Name 'Kompany'

Choosing a name for the band was a significant milestone. They wanted something that encapsulated their spirit and camaraderie. After much deliberation, they settled on "Kompany." The spelling was a nod to their unique identity, while the meaning reflected their belief in the power of togetherness. They understood that music was not just about individual talent but about creating a collective experience.

The First Rehearsals

The early rehearsals were filled with laughter and the occasional disagreement, but they were crucial in shaping their sound. They experimented with different instruments, melodies, and lyrics, often recording their sessions to track their progress. The act of creating together was exhilarating, and it fostered a sense of unity that would carry them through the years.

As they honed their skills, they began to write their own songs, drawing inspiration from their lives and the world around them. The lyrics often reflected their dreams, fears, and the stories of their youth. Each song was a chapter in their collective narrative, a testament to their growth as musicians and friends.

The Dream Becomes Reality

The moment that truly marked the birth of Kompany was when they played their first original song at a local venue. The audience's reaction was overwhelming, and it solidified their belief that they were meant to do this. It was a dream come true, a culmination of years of friendship, hard work, and dedication.

This pivotal performance led to more opportunities, including collaborations with other local artists and invitations to play at larger venues. The dream was no longer just a distant thought; it was becoming a reality. The equation of their success could be represented as:

$$R = P + O + D \tag{4}$$

where R is the realization of their dream, P represents their passion, O denotes the opportunities they seized, and D symbolizes the dedication they poured into their craft.

Conclusion

In the tapestry of their journey, the birth of Kompany stands as a vibrant thread, woven with the colors of friendship, passion, and resilience. It was a dream that transformed into reality, not just for the band but for every fan who believed in their music. As they embarked on this journey, they knew that they were not just creating songs; they were building a legacy that would resonate for years to come. The heartbeat of Kompany had begun, and it echoed the dreams of every young musician who dared to dream big.

Chapter One: A Journey Begins

The Early Days

Finding their sound

The journey of a band often begins with the exploration of its unique musical identity—a quest that is both exhilarating and fraught with challenges. For Kompany, this phase was characterized by a blend of influences, experimentation, and a relentless pursuit of authenticity.

In the early days, the members of Kompany, who had been childhood friends, found themselves navigating the diverse landscape of musical genres. Each member brought their own influences to the table, creating a rich tapestry of sounds that would ultimately define their style. The band drew inspiration from various genres, including rock, pop, and folk, incorporating elements that resonated with their individual tastes and experiences.

One of the primary challenges faced during this formative period was the convergence of differing musical backgrounds. For instance, while one member may have been deeply rooted in classic rock, another might have leaned towards contemporary pop. This divergence necessitated a process of negotiation and compromise, as the band sought to create a cohesive sound that represented all of their artistic visions.

To facilitate this exploration, the band engaged in a series of jam sessions, where they could experiment with different chord progressions, rhythms, and melodies. These sessions were crucial in allowing them to discover their collective voice. A notable example of this was when they stumbled upon a particular chord progression that resonated with them—an emotive sequence that would later become the foundation for their breakout hit.

Theoretical frameworks in music can provide insight into this process. The concept of *tonal harmony*—the relationship between different chords and keys—played a significant role in shaping their sound. The band experimented with various harmonic structures, often utilizing the circle of fifths to explore key changes that added depth to their compositions. For example, transitioning from the key of C major to A minor introduced a contrasting emotional quality that they found appealing.

Moreover, the band faced the challenge of *stylistic coherence*. While experimentation was key, they needed to ensure that their sound did not become disjointed. To address this, they established a set of guiding principles that would inform their songwriting. These principles included a focus on lyrical storytelling, melodic hooks, and rhythmic drive. By adhering to these guidelines, they were able to maintain a sense of unity in their music while still exploring diverse influences.

As they honed their sound, they began to draw from their personal experiences, infusing their lyrics with authenticity. This lyrical depth not only resonated with their audience but also set them apart in a crowded music scene. They tackled themes of love, loss, and self-discovery, crafting narratives that spoke to the human experience. An example of this is found in their early song "Echoes of Yesterday," which combined poignant lyrics with a haunting melody, encapsulating the bittersweet nature of nostalgia.

The process of finding their sound was not without its setbacks. There were moments of frustration when a song did not come together as envisioned, leading to self-doubt among the members. However, these challenges ultimately served as opportunities for growth. They learned to embrace the imperfections in their music, understanding that vulnerability could be a powerful tool for connection with their audience.

In conclusion, the phase of finding their sound was a pivotal moment in Kompany's journey. It was marked by exploration, experimentation, and a commitment to authenticity. Through collaborative efforts and a willingness to confront challenges, they began to carve out a unique musical identity that would resonate with listeners and lay the groundwork for their future success. This foundational period not only shaped their sound but also solidified their bond as a band, setting the stage for the remarkable journey that lay ahead.

The first gigs and local recognition

The journey of Kompany began in the vibrant heart of their hometown, where the rhythm of life pulsated with a unique energy. As childhood friends, they shared not only a bond of friendship but also a fervent passion for music that had been nurtured since their early years. This passion ignited their desire to perform live, leading them to seek out opportunities to showcase their sound in front of an audience.

The Early Performances

Their first gigs were humble affairs, often held in local cafes and community events. The excitement was palpable as they took the stage, instruments in hand, hearts racing with anticipation. These early performances were characterized by a sense of raw authenticity, where the band poured their souls into every note. They played a mix of original songs and covers, aiming to connect with the audience while also honing their craft.

$$E = mc^2 \tag{5}$$

This equation, famously attributed to Einstein, symbolizes the energy they brought to each performance, where E represents the emotional connection they sought to create with their audience, m represents the music they played, and c represents the speed of sound — a metaphor for how quickly their sound would resonate with listeners.

Local Recognition

As they continued to perform, word began to spread about the band's unique sound and energetic performances. Local music enthusiasts started to take notice, and soon enough, they found themselves playing at larger venues. Their ability to engage with the crowd, coupled with their growing repertoire of original songs, garnered them a loyal following.

The band's breakthrough came when they were invited to perform at a well-known local music festival. This was a pivotal moment that marked their transition from obscurity to local fame. The festival provided them with a platform to reach a wider audience, and their performance was met with enthusiastic applause.

Challenges Faced

However, the road to recognition was not without its challenges. They faced fierce competition from other local acts, each vying for the attention of the same audience. The pressure to stand out in a crowded music scene was immense. There were nights when the turnout was disappointing, and self-doubt began to creep in.

During one particularly challenging gig, where only a handful of people showed up, the band experienced a moment of introspection. They realized that their love for music was the driving force behind their performances, not the size of the audience. This epiphany fueled their determination to continue pushing forward, regardless of the obstacles they faced.

Building a Loyal Fan Base

Through relentless dedication and a commitment to their craft, Kompany gradually built a loyal fan base. They engaged with their fans on social media, sharing behind-the-scenes glimpses of their journey and inviting feedback on their music. This interaction fostered a sense of community and belonging, making fans feel like they were part of the band's story.

The band's growing popularity was also aided by their collaborations with other local artists. These partnerships not only enriched their musical experience but also expanded their reach within the local music scene. Each collaboration brought a fresh perspective, allowing Kompany to experiment with different genres and styles, further solidifying their identity as a band.

Recognition from Local Media

As their reputation grew, so did the attention from local media. Music blogs and radio stations began to feature their songs, and interviews followed. This newfound visibility helped to elevate their status within the community. They were no longer just a group of friends playing in small venues; they were becoming recognized artists with a unique sound that resonated with many.

The culmination of their early efforts was a feature article in a popular local magazine, which highlighted their journey and aspirations. This recognition not only validated their hard work but also inspired them to aim higher.

Conclusion

In summary, the first gigs and local recognition were crucial in shaping the identity of Kompany. These formative experiences taught them the importance of resilience, community, and the power of music to connect people. As they moved forward, the lessons learned during this phase would serve as a foundation for their future endeavors, propelling them toward greater heights in their musical journey.

Challenges and setbacks

The journey of Kompany, like that of many aspiring musicians, was not without its share of challenges and setbacks. As they embarked on their musical voyage, the band faced numerous obstacles that tested their resolve and commitment to their craft. These challenges can be categorized into three primary areas: financial constraints, interpersonal conflicts, and the struggle for artistic identity.

Financial Constraints

In the early days, financial stability was a significant hurdle for Kompany. The costs associated with rehearsals, recording, and promoting their music often exceeded their meager budgets. This financial strain led to a critical equation for the band:

$$\text{Total Costs} = \text{Rehearsal Expenses} + \text{Recording Costs} + \text{Promotion Fees} \qquad (6)$$

Where: - Rehearsal Expenses included studio rentals and equipment. - Recording Costs encompassed studio time and producer fees. - Promotion Fees involved marketing materials and social media advertising.

To mitigate these costs, the band relied heavily on grassroots fundraising efforts, including local gigs and merchandise sales. For instance, they organized benefit concerts, where ticket sales would go directly towards funding their next recording session. Despite their efforts, the financial pressure often led to stress and anxiety, which could have derailed their ambitions.

Interpersonal Conflicts

As childhood friends, the members of Kompany shared a deep bond, but this closeness also made them vulnerable to interpersonal conflicts. Differences in artistic vision and creative direction often sparked heated debates. For example, when it came to selecting songs for their first album, disagreements arose regarding the blend of genres and the overall sound. One member might advocate for a more pop-oriented approach, while another pushed for a raw, indie vibe.

These conflicts can be represented by the following model of communication breakdown:

$$\text{Conflict} = \text{Miscommunication} + \text{Differing Goals} + \text{Emotional Stress} \qquad (7)$$

To address these tensions, the band implemented regular meetings where each member could express their views openly. This practice not only fostered a sense of collaboration but also allowed them to navigate their differences constructively. The ability to compromise became crucial, as they learned that each member's contribution was vital to the band's overall success.

Struggle for Artistic Identity

Kompany also faced the daunting task of carving out their unique artistic identity in a saturated music market. As they began to gain traction, they were often compared to established bands, leading to an internal struggle over their sound. The pressure to conform to industry standards sometimes overshadowed their original vision, creating a conflict between authenticity and commercial viability.

This struggle can be illustrated through the following relationship:

$$\text{Artistic Identity} = \text{Authenticity} - \text{Commercial Pressure} \qquad (8)$$

To navigate this challenge, the band decided to experiment with different styles and genres, drawing from their diverse musical influences. They spent countless hours in the studio, blending elements of rock, pop, and folk to create a sound that was distinctly their own. This experimentation not only helped them discover their artistic voice but also resonated with their growing fan base.

Conclusion

Despite the myriad of challenges and setbacks, Kompany's resilience and determination shone through. The financial constraints forced them to be resourceful, the interpersonal conflicts taught them the importance of communication and compromise, and the struggle for artistic identity ultimately led them to discover their unique sound. These experiences, while difficult, were instrumental in shaping the band into the powerhouse they would become, laying a solid foundation for their future successes.

Rise to Local Fame

Breaking into the local music scene

The journey of Kompany into the local music scene was not just a mere entry; it was a heartfelt plunge into the depths of creativity, community, and the raw, unfiltered essence of music. Emerging from the small, tight-knit community where they honed their craft, the band faced both exhilarating opportunities and daunting challenges that would shape their identity and sound.

Understanding the Local Music Landscape

To break into the local music scene, Kompany first needed to understand the intricate dynamics of their environment. The local scene was a tapestry woven from diverse influences, genres, and artistic expressions. It was essential for the band to identify their niche within this vibrant ecosystem. According to [1], a successful entry into any music scene requires an understanding of the following elements:

- **Audience Demographics:** Knowing who listens to what, and where their interests lie.

- **Venue Selection:** Identifying the right venues that align with their musical style and target audience.

- **Networking:** Building relationships with local musicians, promoters, and venue owners.

Kompany immersed themselves in the local music culture, attending shows, participating in open mic nights, and engaging with other artists. This grassroots approach not only helped them understand the scene but also allowed them to build a supportive network that would prove invaluable in their journey.

First Gigs and Local Recognition

The first gigs were pivotal moments for Kompany. They played at small bars and community events, where the atmosphere was intimate, and the audience was often comprised of friends and family. These initial performances were fraught with nerves but also filled with a sense of belonging. The band quickly learned that every performance was an opportunity to refine their sound and stage presence.

During these early shows, Kompany experimented with their setlist, often incorporating covers of popular songs alongside their original compositions. This strategy served two purposes: it attracted a wider audience and showcased their musical versatility. As they gained traction, local media outlets began to take notice. A review in the *Local Music Gazette* highlighted their energetic performances and unique sound, which blended elements of rock, pop, and folk.

Challenges and Setbacks

Despite their growing popularity, the path to local fame was not without its challenges. One of the most significant hurdles was the fierce competition within the local scene. Numerous bands were vying for the same venues and audience attention, leading to a saturated market. To stand out, Kompany had to develop a distinctive brand identity. This involved not only their musical style but also their visual presentation and engagement with fans.

Another challenge was the technical aspects of performing live. Early on, they encountered issues with sound equipment, stage fright, and the logistics of organizing their performances. These setbacks were frustrating but also served as valuable learning experiences. The band adopted a philosophy of resilience, viewing each obstacle as a stepping stone rather than a roadblock. This mindset is supported by [2], who posits that resilience in creative fields is crucial for long-term success.

Building a Loyal Fan Base

As Kompany continued to perform, they began to cultivate a loyal fan base. This was achieved through consistent engagement with their audience both on and off the stage. They utilized social media platforms to share behind-the-scenes content, upcoming shows, and personal stories, fostering a sense of community among their followers. This direct connection with fans created a supportive environment where listeners felt personally invested in the band's journey.

The band also recognized the importance of feedback. After shows, they would often interact with fans, asking for their thoughts on the performance and what songs resonated most. This practice not only provided valuable insights but also strengthened the bond between the band and their audience.

Collaborations and Musical Partnerships

In their quest to break into the local music scene, Kompany understood the power of collaboration. They reached out to other local artists for joint performances, which not only expanded their audience but also enriched their musical repertoire. Collaborations with other musicians allowed them to explore new sounds and styles, enhancing their creativity.

One notable partnership was with a local singer-songwriter, whose acoustic style complemented Kompany's energetic performances. Together, they created a series of shows that attracted larger crowds and garnered positive reviews. This collaboration exemplified the idea that in the music industry, "a rising tide lifts all boats," as articulated by [3].

Conclusion

Breaking into the local music scene was a multifaceted journey for Kompany, characterized by a blend of passion, perseverance, and community engagement. Through understanding their audience, overcoming challenges, and building relationships, they established themselves as a formidable presence in the local music landscape. This foundational phase not only set the stage for their future successes but also instilled in them the values of resilience, collaboration, and connection that would guide them throughout their career.

The lessons learned during this period would resonate deeply as they transitioned from local favorites to national sensations, but it was in those intimate, crowded bars and community events where the heart of Kompany truly began to beat.

Bibliography

[1] Smith, J. (2020). *Understanding Local Music Scenes*. New York: Music Press.

[2] Johnson, A. (2019). *Resilience in the Creative Arts*. London: Creative Minds Publishing.

[3] Lee, R. (2021). *The Power of Collaboration in Music*. Los Angeles: Harmony Books.

Building a loyal fan base

Building a loyal fan base is essential for any band aspiring to achieve long-term success in the music industry. For Kompany, this process was not merely a byproduct of their musical journey; it was a calculated and heartfelt endeavor that involved nurturing relationships, engaging with fans, and creating memorable experiences. This section delves into the strategies employed by Kompany, the challenges they faced, and the theoretical frameworks that underpin effective fan engagement.

Theoretical Frameworks

To understand how Kompany built their loyal fan base, it is useful to explore several theories related to fan engagement and loyalty. One such theory is the **Social Identity Theory**, which posits that individuals derive part of their self-concept from their membership in social groups. For fans, identifying with a band can enhance their self-esteem and provide a sense of belonging. Kompany capitalized on this by fostering a community where fans felt like they were part of something larger than themselves.

Another relevant framework is the **Commitment-Trust Theory**, which emphasizes the importance of trust and commitment in relationships. By consistently engaging with their fans and showing appreciation for their support,

Kompany was able to cultivate a strong sense of loyalty. This theory suggests that when fans trust a band and feel committed to its values, they are more likely to remain loyal over time.

Strategies for Engagement

Kompany employed several strategies to build and maintain their fan base:

1. Authenticity and Relatability From the very beginning, Kompany prioritized authenticity in their music and interactions. Their lyrics often reflected personal experiences and emotions, allowing fans to relate on a deeper level. By sharing their struggles and triumphs, they created a bond with their audience that transcended mere admiration for their music. This authenticity resonated with fans, fostering a sense of loyalty that was rooted in genuine connection.

2. Social Media Presence In the digital age, social media has become a vital tool for artists to connect with their fans. Kompany embraced platforms such as Instagram, Twitter, and Facebook to share behind-the-scenes content, engage in conversations, and respond to fan inquiries. This direct interaction made fans feel valued and heard, reinforcing their loyalty to the band. The equation for engagement can be simplified as:

$$E = C + I + R \qquad (9)$$

where E is engagement, C is connection, I is interaction, and R is response. By maximizing these components, Kompany effectively increased their engagement levels.

3. Memorable Live Performances Live performances are a powerful way to create lasting memories with fans. Kompany understood that each concert was an opportunity to deepen their connection with their audience. They crafted setlists that included fan favorites and often encouraged audience participation. The energy of a live show, combined with the emotional weight of their music, left fans with unforgettable experiences that solidified their loyalty.

4. Exclusive Content and Merchandise Offering exclusive content and merchandise is another effective strategy for building a loyal fan base. Kompany launched a membership program that provided fans with early access to new music, exclusive behind-the-scenes videos, and limited-edition merchandise. This not only rewarded loyal fans but also created a sense of exclusivity that made them feel special. The perceived value of exclusivity can be illustrated through the following equation:

$$P = V - C \qquad (10)$$

where P is perceived value, V is the value of the exclusive content, and C is the cost of acquiring it. By maximizing V and minimizing C, Kompany enhanced the perceived value of their offerings.

Challenges Faced

Despite their success in building a loyal fan base, Kompany encountered several challenges along the way. One significant issue was the saturation of the music market. With numerous emerging artists vying for attention, standing out became increasingly difficult. Kompany addressed this challenge by differentiating themselves through their unique sound and authentic storytelling, ensuring that they remained memorable in the minds of their fans.

Another challenge was managing fan expectations. As the band gained popularity, fans often developed lofty expectations for new music and performances. Kompany navigated this by maintaining open lines of communication, expressing their commitment to quality over quantity, and emphasizing their creative process. This transparency helped mitigate disappointment and reinforced trust among their fan base.

Conclusion

In conclusion, building a loyal fan base is a multifaceted endeavor that requires authenticity, engagement, and strategic communication. Kompany's success in this area can be attributed to their genuine connection with fans, effective use of social media, memorable live performances, and exclusive offerings. By understanding the theoretical frameworks that underpin fan loyalty and addressing the challenges they faced, Kompany not only built a dedicated following but also established a lasting legacy in the music industry. Their journey serves as a testament to the power of genuine relationships and the impact of meaningful engagement in creating a loyal fan base.

Collaborations and Musical Partnerships

The journey of Kompany was not solely defined by their individual talents, but rather by the vibrant tapestry woven through collaborations and partnerships that enriched their sound and expanded their reach. In the world of music, collaboration serves as a powerful catalyst for creativity, allowing artists to blend diverse influences and styles. For Kompany, these partnerships became instrumental in their rise to local fame and beyond.

The Importance of Collaboration

Collaboration in music can often lead to innovative outcomes that would be difficult to achieve in isolation. As noted by [1], collaborative efforts can result in a synergy where the combined output is greater than the sum of its parts. This principle can be represented mathematically as:

$$C = A + B + (A \times B) \tag{11}$$

where C represents the collaborative output, A and B represent the individual contributions of each collaborator, and the term $A \times B$ accounts for the synergistic effect of their combined efforts.

Kompany embraced this philosophy wholeheartedly, seeking out musicians, producers, and songwriters who could complement their unique sound. Their collaborations not only diversified their musical palette but also introduced them to new audiences, broadening their fan base.

Key Collaborations

One of the pivotal moments in Kompany's journey occurred during their collaboration with local producer and musician, Jamie Lee. Jamie, known for his eclectic style and innovative production techniques, brought a fresh perspective to Kompany's songwriting process. The partnership yielded the hit single "Echoes of Tomorrow," which showcased an experimental blend of electronic beats and acoustic melodies. This track not only topped local charts but also caught the attention of national radio stations, marking a significant turning point in their career.

In addition to working with producers, Kompany also sought out fellow musicians for joint projects. Their collaboration with indie rock band, The Dreamers, resulted in the powerful anthem "Together We Rise." This song highlighted the themes of unity and resilience, resonating deeply with fans during a time of social upheaval. The partnership exemplified how collaborative efforts could amplify messages and create a deeper emotional connection with listeners.

Challenges in Collaboration

Despite the numerous benefits, collaborations also presented challenges. Different artistic visions could lead to creative friction, as each member brought their own ideas and preferences to the table. For instance, during the recording sessions for their second album, tensions arose between Kompany and a guest artist, leading to disagreements over song arrangements and lyrical content. This situation required open communication and compromise, emphasizing the importance of maintaining a collaborative spirit even amidst conflict.

As [2] suggests, effective conflict resolution strategies, such as active listening and finding common ground, are essential in collaborative environments. Kompany learned to navigate these challenges, ultimately emerging stronger and more united as a band.

The Impact of Collaborations on Kompany's Sound

Through their collaborations, Kompany was able to evolve their musical style, incorporating elements from various genres including rock, pop, and electronic music. This genre-blending approach not only set them apart from their contemporaries but also attracted a diverse audience. Their willingness to experiment with different sounds is a testament to the power of collaboration in fostering artistic growth.

For example, their partnership with electronic artist, Zara K, led to the creation of the track "Neon Dreams," which featured pulsating synths and ethereal vocals. This song marked a departure from their earlier work and showcased their ability to adapt and innovate within the ever-changing music landscape.

Conclusion

In summary, the collaborations and musical partnerships that Kompany engaged in were pivotal to their development as artists. These relationships not only enhanced their creative output but also facilitated their growth within the music industry. By embracing collaboration, Kompany demonstrated that the journey of music is not a solitary path but a shared experience that thrives on connection and community.

Bibliography

[1] Author, A. (Year). *The Art of Collaboration in Music*. Publisher.

[2] Author, B. (Year). *Navigating Creative Conflicts: Strategies for Success*. Publisher.

The Road to the First Album

Songwriting process and experimentation

The songwriting process for Kompany has always been a blend of creativity, collaboration, and experimentation. Each member brought their unique influences and experiences to the table, creating a rich tapestry of sound that defined their early work. This section delves into the intricacies of their songwriting journey, exploring the methods they employed, the challenges they faced, and the innovative approaches that shaped their music.

Collaborative Writing

At the heart of Kompany's songwriting process is collaboration. The band members often gathered in informal settings, such as living rooms or local cafes, to share ideas and melodies. This collaborative spirit was crucial in fostering an environment where creativity could flourish. The use of brainstorming sessions allowed them to explore various themes and concepts, often leading to unexpected lyrical directions.

For instance, during one such session, a simple chord progression played by the guitarist inspired a lyrical exploration of heartbreak. The spontaneous nature of these gatherings often resulted in songs that felt genuine and relatable. The band believed that the synergy of their collective experiences enriched their music, making it resonate deeply with their audience.

Experimentation with Genres

Kompany's early songwriting was marked by a willingness to experiment with various genres. Drawing inspiration from pop, rock, and even elements of folk, they sought to create a sound that was distinctly their own. This genre-blending approach allowed them to push the boundaries of traditional songwriting.

An example of this experimentation can be seen in their track *"Chasing Shadows"*, where they combined a folk-inspired acoustic guitar riff with electronic beats. This fusion not only showcased their versatility but also attracted a diverse fan base. The band's willingness to step outside their comfort zone was instrumental in shaping their identity and sound.

The Role of Technology

As technology advanced, so did Kompany's songwriting process. The introduction of digital audio workstations (DAWs) revolutionized how they created music. With software such as Ableton Live and Logic Pro, the band could experiment with sounds and arrangements in ways that were previously unimaginable.

Using these tools, they could layer tracks, manipulate audio, and incorporate samples into their songs. This technological integration allowed for a more dynamic songwriting process. For example, the song *"Electric Dreams"* was born from a simple synth loop created in the studio, which led to the exploration of themes related to technology and modern love.

Lyrical Themes and Structures

Kompany's lyrics often reflect personal experiences and societal observations. Their songwriting process involved a deep dive into themes such as love, loss, and self-discovery. The band members would often draw from their own lives, transforming raw emotions into powerful lyrics.

In terms of structure, they experimented with traditional verse-chorus forms, often incorporating bridges and pre-choruses to create tension and release. This experimentation with song structure not only kept their music engaging but also allowed them to tell compelling stories. For instance, in the song *"Breaking Free"*, the bridge serves as a moment of reflection before the explosive final chorus, enhancing the emotional impact of the track.

Challenges in the Process

Despite their creative successes, Kompany faced several challenges during their songwriting journey. One significant issue was writer's block, a common hurdle for many artists. To combat this, the band developed strategies to reignite their creativity, such as taking breaks, seeking inspiration from other art forms, or collaborating with outside writers.

Additionally, the pressure of creating commercially viable music sometimes led to conflicts within the band. Balancing artistic integrity with the expectations of the music industry was a constant struggle. However, these challenges ultimately strengthened their resolve and fostered a deeper understanding of their artistic vision.

Conclusion

The songwriting process for Kompany was not just about crafting songs; it was a journey of exploration, collaboration, and innovation. Through their willingness to experiment with genres, embrace technology, and tackle personal and societal themes, they carved out a unique space in the music landscape. The challenges they faced only served to deepen their connection to their art and to one another, laying the foundation for their future successes.

Recording studios and producers

The journey of creating an album is an intricate tapestry woven with threads of creativity, technical expertise, and emotional investment. For Kompany, the recording process was not merely a phase of production; it was a transformative experience that shaped their sound and identity as artists. In this section, we delve into the pivotal role of recording studios and producers in crafting the sonic landscape of their first album.

Choosing the Right Studio

Selecting a recording studio is akin to choosing a sanctuary for an artist's soul. It is where raw ideas are sculpted into polished tracks, and the atmosphere can significantly impact the creative process. For Kompany, the decision was influenced by several factors:

- **Acoustic Environment:** The studio's acoustics play a crucial role in capturing the essence of sound. Studios with high-quality soundproofing and acoustically treated rooms ensure that the recordings are free from unwanted noise and reverberation. Kompany opted for a studio renowned for its vibrant acoustic environment, which allowed them to explore a range of sounds and textures.

- **Equipment and Technology:** The availability of state-of-the-art recording equipment is paramount. From high-fidelity microphones to advanced mixing consoles, the tools of the trade can make or break a recording session. Kompany sought out a studio equipped with vintage and modern gear, allowing them to experiment with various recording techniques.

- **Producer Expertise:** A producer's vision and experience can significantly shape the final product. Kompany was fortunate to collaborate with a producer who not only understood their musical style but also pushed them to explore new directions. This synergy between the band and the producer was essential in realizing their artistic vision.

The Recording Process

The recording sessions for Kompany's first album were characterized by a mix of excitement and anxiety. As they stepped into the studio, they were greeted by the hum of machinery and the comforting presence of their producer. The process unfolded in several stages:

1. **Pre-Production:** Before the recording began, the band engaged in extensive pre-production sessions. This involved refining song structures, experimenting with arrangements, and discussing the overall sound they wanted to achieve. The producer facilitated these discussions, ensuring that each member's voice was heard.

2. **Tracking:** The tracking phase involved laying down the foundational elements of each song. This typically began with the rhythm section—drums and bass—followed by guitars, keyboards, and vocals. Each instrument was recorded separately to allow for greater control during the mixing process. Kompany found this phase exhilarating, as they could hear their songs come to life in real-time.

3. **Layering and Overdubs:** Once the basic tracks were laid down, the band entered the layering phase. This involved adding additional instruments, harmonies, and effects to enrich the sound. The producer encouraged experimentation, leading to unexpected sonic discoveries. For instance, a

simple guitar riff evolved into a lush soundscape with the addition of strings and backing vocals.

4. **Mixing:** After all the tracks were recorded, the mixing process began. This is where the magic truly happens, as the producer balances levels, applies effects, and creates a cohesive sound. Kompany spent hours in the mixing suite, fine-tuning each element to ensure that the final product reflected their artistic intent. The mixing process also involved discussions about dynamics, panning, and the overall sonic palette.

5. **Mastering:** The final step in the recording process was mastering, where the mixed tracks were polished for distribution. This stage involved adjusting the overall volume, equalization, and compression to ensure that the album would sound great on various playback systems. Kompany learned the importance of mastering in achieving a professional sound, as it can dramatically affect how music is perceived by listeners.

Challenges Faced

While the recording process is often romanticized, it is not without its challenges. Kompany encountered several obstacles that tested their resilience and creativity:

- **Time Constraints:** The pressure of studio time can be daunting. With limited hours booked, the band often felt rushed to complete recordings. This led to moments of frustration, but they learned to focus on efficiency without sacrificing creativity.

- **Creative Differences:** Collaborating closely with a producer can sometimes lead to creative tensions. Kompany experienced disagreements regarding song arrangements and production choices. Through open communication and compromise, they navigated these challenges, ultimately strengthening their bond as a band.

- **Technical Issues:** No recording session is immune to technical difficulties. From equipment malfunctions to software glitches, Kompany faced their fair share of setbacks. However, these moments often led to improvisation and unexpected creative breakthroughs.

Examples of Influential Producers

Kompany drew inspiration from several influential producers throughout their journey. Understanding the impact of a producer's vision can provide insight into the creative process:

- **Rick Rubin:** Known for his eclectic approach, Rubin has worked with artists across genres. His ability to strip down songs to their essence resonated with Kompany, encouraging them to focus on the core of their music.

- **Max Martin:** A master of pop production, Martin's knack for crafting catchy hooks and polished soundscapes influenced Kompany's desire to create memorable melodies that would resonate with listeners.

- **T-Bone Burnett:** Burnett's emphasis on authenticity and organic sound inspired Kompany to incorporate live instrumentation and raw emotion into their recordings, resulting in a more genuine representation of their artistry.

Conclusion

The recording studios and producers that Kompany collaborated with played a pivotal role in shaping their first album. The blend of creativity, technical expertise, and emotional investment culminated in a body of work that not only showcased their musical talents but also resonated deeply with their audience. Through challenges and triumphs, the journey of recording became a defining chapter in the story of Kompany, laying the foundation for their future successes in the music industry.

Overcoming obstacles and setbacks

The journey of Kompany was not without its fair share of challenges and obstacles. As the band ventured into the recording studio to create their first album, they encountered a myriad of difficulties that tested their resolve and unity. This section delves into the various hurdles they faced and the strategies they employed to overcome them.

Creative Differences

One of the most significant challenges the band faced was navigating creative differences among its members. Each member brought a unique perspective and style to the table, which, while enriching the band's sound, often led to disagreements on song direction and arrangement. For instance, during the writing sessions for their first album, tensions arose when one member favored a more experimental sound, while another preferred a classic rock approach.

To address these differences, the band implemented a collaborative framework, which included regular brainstorming sessions where each member could present their ideas without judgment. This approach allowed them to blend various influences into a cohesive sound. The equation for successful collaboration can be expressed as:

$$C = \frac{I_1 + I_2 + I_3 + ... + I_n}{N}$$

Where C represents the collaborative output, I_i represents the individual contributions, and N is the number of members. By fostering an environment of respect and open communication, Kompany was able to transform their differences into a strength, ultimately leading to a richer and more diverse musical palette.

Financial Constraints

Another significant obstacle was the financial constraints that often accompany the early stages of a band's career. With limited budgets for recording, marketing, and touring, Kompany had to be resourceful. They relied heavily on crowdfunding campaigns and local sponsorships to finance their debut album. The band organized benefit concerts, where ticket sales and merchandise proceeds were directed towards their recording fund.

This grassroots approach not only alleviated financial pressure but also strengthened their bond with the local community. The equation illustrating the relationship between community support and financial viability can be expressed as:

$$F = S \cdot C$$

Where F is the financial support, S is the strength of community engagement, and C is the level of local interest in the band. By actively engaging their fanbase and demonstrating their commitment to the local music scene, Kompany was able to secure the necessary funds to produce their first album.

Technical Challenges

The technical challenges associated with recording were another hurdle. The band faced issues ranging from subpar recording equipment to inexperienced sound engineers. In one particularly frustrating session, a power outage caused them to lose several hours of work, leading to feelings of despair and frustration.

To overcome these technical setbacks, Kompany sought the expertise of seasoned professionals in the industry. They reached out to established producers and sound engineers who could offer guidance and support. This decision proved to be pivotal, as it not only improved the quality of their recordings but also provided valuable learning experiences for the band members. The relationship between professional mentorship and artistic growth can be described by the following equation:

$$G = M \cdot E$$

Where G represents artistic growth, M denotes the quality of mentorship, and E is the effort put in by the band members to learn and adapt. By investing time in building relationships with industry veterans, Kompany was able to enhance their technical skills and improve their overall sound.

Personal Struggles

Beyond the professional challenges, personal struggles also threatened to derail the band's progress. Balancing personal relationships, mental health, and the demands of a burgeoning music career proved to be a delicate act. Members faced issues such as anxiety, burnout, and the strain of maintaining personal relationships while pursuing their dreams.

Recognizing the importance of mental health, the band made a collective decision to prioritize self-care. They implemented regular check-ins to discuss not only their musical progress but also their emotional well-being. This proactive approach fostered a supportive environment where members felt comfortable sharing their struggles. The equation that encapsulates the relationship between mental health and performance can be expressed as:

$$P = \frac{M}{W}$$

Where P is performance, M is mental health, and W is workload. By managing their workload and ensuring that each member felt supported, Kompany was able to maintain a high level of creativity and productivity.

Conclusion

Through these various obstacles—creative differences, financial constraints, technical challenges, and personal struggles—Kompany demonstrated resilience and adaptability. Their ability to confront and overcome these setbacks not only solidified their bond as a band but also laid the groundwork for their future success. The lessons learned during this tumultuous period would prove invaluable as they continued their journey in the music industry, ultimately leading to the creation of their breakthrough album that would change everything.

In retrospect, the struggles they faced were not merely hindrances but rather essential components of their growth as artists and as individuals. Each challenge served as a stepping stone, propelling them forward on their path to success and solidifying their commitment to their music and each other.

Chapter Highlights:

The breakthrough hit that changed everything

In the world of music, a breakthrough hit can serve as the catalyst that propels a band from obscurity to national prominence. For Kompany, this pivotal moment came with the release of their single *"Echoes of Tomorrow"*, a track that not only showcased their unique sound but also resonated deeply with audiences across the country.

The Songwriting Process

The creation of *"Echoes of Tomorrow"* was an intricate process that involved collaboration among all band members. The songwriting sessions were characterized by a blend of individual creativity and collective brainstorming. According to music theory, successful songwriting often follows a structure that includes elements such as verse, chorus, and bridge. Kompany utilized the following structure for their hit:

$$SongStructure = Verse + Chorus + Verse + Chorus + Bridge + Chorus \tag{12}$$

The verses of the song delve into themes of nostalgia and hope, while the chorus serves as an anthemic call to action, encouraging listeners to embrace change.

Musical Influences

Musically, the band drew inspiration from various genres, including pop, rock, and elements of folk. This eclectic mix is evident in the instrumentation and arrangement of the song. The use of a driving guitar riff, layered harmonies, and a powerful drumbeat created a rich soundscape that captivated listeners.

The harmonic progression followed a common pop structure, which can be represented as:

$$ChordProgression = I - V - vi - IV \tag{13}$$

This progression is known for its emotional resonance and is frequently used in chart-topping hits.

Recording and Production

The recording process took place in a renowned studio, where the band worked closely with a seasoned producer. The producer's role was crucial in shaping the final sound of *"Echoes of Tomorrow"*. Utilizing advanced recording techniques, they captured the raw energy of the band's performance while ensuring that each instrument was balanced perfectly in the mix.

One of the notable challenges during the recording was achieving the right vocal production. The band experimented with various vocal effects, such as reverb and delay, to enhance the emotional impact of the lyrics. The final mix employed the following formula for achieving a polished sound:

$$FinalMix = (Vocals + Instruments) \times (Effects + Mastering) \tag{14}$$

This approach ensured that the song was radio-ready and appealing to a broad audience.

Release and Reception

Upon its release, *"Echoes of Tomorrow"* quickly gained traction on social media platforms and music streaming services. The accompanying music video, featuring stunning visuals that complemented the song's themes, further propelled its popularity. Within weeks, the single climbed the charts, eventually reaching the top ten on the national music charts.

The song's success was not just a result of its musical composition but also of strategic marketing efforts. The band launched a targeted campaign that included interviews, live performances, and social media engagement, which helped create a buzz around the release.

Impact on Kompany's Career

The impact of *"Echoes of Tomorrow"* on Kompany's career was profound. It marked a turning point, leading to increased media attention, invitations to perform at major music festivals, and opportunities to collaborate with established artists. The single not only solidified their place in the music industry but also connected them with a loyal fan base that resonated with the song's message.

In the wake of this breakthrough hit, the band found themselves navigating the complexities of newfound fame. They faced the pressures of living up to expectations while striving to maintain their creative integrity. The success of *"Echoes of Tomorrow"* served as both a blessing and a challenge, pushing them to evolve as artists and explore new musical directions.

Conclusion

Ultimately, *"Echoes of Tomorrow"* was more than just a song; it was a defining moment for Kompany. It encapsulated their journey, their struggles, and their aspirations. The breakthrough hit not only changed everything for the band but also left an indelible mark on the music landscape, inspiring countless aspiring musicians to chase their dreams. As they moved forward, the echoes of their past would continue to resonate, reminding them of the power of music to transform lives and create connections.

First taste of national recognition

As the echoes of their early performances began to fade into the background, Kompany found themselves on the precipice of something monumental—a moment that would catapult them from the cozy confines of their local scene into the vast expanse of national recognition. This transition, while exhilarating, was not without its complexities and challenges.

The journey toward national acclaim began with the release of their first single, *"Chasing Shadows"*. This track was not just a collection of notes and lyrics; it was a heartfelt expression of their collective experiences, struggles, and aspirations. The songwriting process was intense, marked by late-night jam sessions and heated discussions about the direction of their sound. As they crafted the song, they drew inspiration from a myriad of influences, weaving together elements of rock, pop, and soul to create a sound that was distinctly their own.

$$\text{Sound} = (\text{Rock} + \text{Pop} + \text{Soul}) \times \text{Emotion} \qquad (15)$$

This equation encapsulates the essence of their music, where the emotional weight of their lyrics was amplified by the fusion of genres. The result was a track that resonated deeply with listeners, capturing the essence of youthful yearning and the quest for identity.

Upon its release, *"Chasing Shadows"* quickly garnered attention on local radio stations. Its infectious melody and relatable lyrics struck a chord with audiences, and soon, requests for the song flooded in. This grassroots support laid the groundwork for their first taste of national recognition. The turning point came when a prominent music blogger featured the single on their website, praising it as "a breath of fresh air in the current music landscape." This endorsement was pivotal; it opened the floodgates for broader media attention.

However, with recognition came scrutiny. The band faced the challenge of maintaining their authenticity amidst the pressures of a growing fanbase and industry expectations. They had to navigate the delicate balance between commercial success and artistic integrity. This struggle is not uncommon in the music industry, where emerging artists often grapple with the fear of losing their unique voice in pursuit of broader appeal.

As they prepared for their first national tour, the pressure intensified. The excitement was palpable, but so was the anxiety. Would they be able to replicate their local success on a larger stage? Would their fans embrace them beyond their hometown? These questions loomed large as they stepped into the recording studio to produce their debut album, *"Reflections"*.

The album's lead single, *"Echoes of Tomorrow"*, was a bold statement of their artistic vision. It showcased their growth as musicians and songwriters, blending poignant lyrics with intricate instrumentation. The release was accompanied by a music video that captured the raw energy of their live performances, further amplifying their presence in the national music scene.

The combination of strategic marketing, social media engagement, and the band's undeniable talent resulted in *"Echoes of Tomorrow"* climbing the charts. It reached the top 20 on several national playlists, marking a significant milestone in their career. This newfound visibility attracted the attention of major record labels, leading to offers that would change the trajectory of Kompany forever.

In the midst of this whirlwind, the band remained grounded. They understood that their journey was just beginning and that national recognition was a double-edged sword. While it brought opportunities, it also heightened expectations. They embraced the support of their loyal fanbase, using social media platforms to connect with listeners and share their experiences. This direct engagement fostered a sense of community, allowing fans to feel like they were part of the journey.

Their first taste of national recognition was not merely an achievement; it was a pivotal moment that solidified their resolve to stay true to their roots. They recognized that while the music industry could be unforgiving, their passion for creating meaningful music would guide them through the challenges ahead. The lessons learned during this time would shape their identity as artists and influence their future endeavors.

As they prepared for their first national tour, the excitement was palpable. Each member of Kompany felt the weight of their dreams on their shoulders, but they also carried the unwavering support of their fans. This collective energy fueled their performances, creating an electric atmosphere at every show. They were no longer just a local band; they were becoming a national sensation, and they were ready to embrace it fully.

In retrospect, the journey from local gigs to national recognition was a testament to their resilience, creativity, and unwavering commitment to their craft. The challenges they faced only strengthened their bond as a band, and the support from their fans served as a reminder of why they started making music in the first place. This chapter in their story was just the beginning, a stepping stone toward a future filled with promise and possibility.

Touring and connecting with fans

As the pulsating heart of Kompany's journey, touring not only served as a means of showcasing their music but also as a vital conduit for forging deep connections with their fans. This chapter of their story is characterized by the electrifying energy of live performances, the intimate exchanges between band and audience, and the profound impact these experiences had on both parties.

The Thrill of Performing Live

The thrill of performing live is an experience that transcends mere entertainment; it is a visceral connection that ignites the very essence of music. For Kompany, each concert became a tapestry woven with the threads of anticipation, excitement, and shared emotion. The theory of *social presence* suggests that individuals feel a heightened sense of connection when they are physically present with others, a phenomenon that is especially pronounced in live music settings.

The band often found themselves on stage, feeling the palpable energy from the crowd. This energy was not just a backdrop; it was a living entity that influenced their performances. According to the *Flow Theory* proposed by Mihaly Csikszentmihalyi, artists experience a state of flow when they are fully immersed in their craft, leading to heightened creativity and satisfaction. During their tours, Kompany members reported experiencing this flow, especially during their most beloved songs, where the synergy between them and the audience reached its peak.

Memorable Tour Moments

Every tour is punctuated with unforgettable moments that become etched in the memories of both the band and their fans. One such moment occurred during a sold-out show at a renowned venue, where the band performed their breakthrough hit. The crowd's response was overwhelming; fans sang every word, creating a chorus that resonated throughout the hall. This moment exemplified the *Audience Participation Theory*, which posits that active engagement enhances the overall experience for both performers and spectators.

Kompany also embraced the notion of spontaneity during their tours. At one show, the lead singer unexpectedly invited a fan on stage to share a duet, creating an intimate experience that left both the fan and the band members in tears. This act not only solidified the bond between them and their audience but also demonstrated the importance of *emotional authenticity* in performance, a concept supported by research indicating that genuine emotional expression fosters stronger connections.

Connecting with Fans on a Deeper Level

Beyond the music, Kompany understood the significance of connecting with their fans on a deeper level. They often engaged in meet-and-greet sessions, allowing fans to share their stories and experiences. This practice aligns with the *Social Exchange Theory*, which posits that relationships are built on the perceived benefits of interaction. By investing time in these connections, Kompany cultivated a loyal fan base that felt valued and appreciated.

One particularly impactful initiative was their "Fan Appreciation Night," held in select cities during their tours. This event featured acoustic performances, Q&A sessions, and personal anecdotes shared by the band. The emotional resonance of these nights was palpable, as fans expressed how Kompany's music had touched their lives during difficult times. Research indicates that music can serve as a powerful tool for emotional regulation, and the band's ability to create a safe space for fans to express their feelings further solidified their bond.

CHAPTER HIGHLIGHTS:

The Challenges of Touring

While touring offered numerous opportunities for connection, it also presented challenges that tested the resilience of Kompany. The grueling schedule, long hours on the road, and the pressures of maintaining a public image often led to exhaustion and stress. The *Burnout Theory* highlights how prolonged exposure to stressors can lead to emotional and physical exhaustion, a reality that the band faced during their most demanding tours.

In one instance, after a particularly intense leg of their tour, the band members experienced a period of disconnection, struggling to maintain their creative synergy. This challenge prompted them to prioritize self-care and mental health, leading to the implementation of wellness practices such as mindfulness and team-building activities. By addressing these challenges head-on, they not only preserved their mental well-being but also strengthened their connection as a band, ultimately enhancing their performances.

The Lasting Impact of Touring

The impact of touring extended far beyond the immediate thrill of live performances. Each concert served as a reminder of the power of music to unite people from diverse backgrounds. Kompany's tours became a celebration of shared experiences, where fans from different walks of life came together, united by a common love for the band's music. This phenomenon aligns with the *Collective Identity Theory*, which suggests that shared experiences can foster a sense of belonging and community among individuals.

In conclusion, touring was not merely a means of promoting their music; it was an integral part of Kompany's identity and legacy. Through the thrill of live performances, memorable moments, and deep connections with fans, the band created a tapestry of experiences that resonated long after the final encore. These connections, forged through music, would become the foundation of their enduring impact on the music industry and the hearts of their fans.

Chapter Two: The Spotlight Shines Brighter

National Success

Signing with a major label

The journey of Kompany reached a pivotal moment when they signed with a major record label, a decision that not only transformed their career trajectory but also reshaped their identity as artists. This section delves into the intricacies of this significant milestone, exploring the theoretical underpinnings of record label dynamics, the challenges they faced, and the profound impact of this partnership on their music and public persona.

Understanding Major Labels

Major labels, often referred to as the "Big Three" in the music industry—Universal Music Group, Sony Music Entertainment, and Warner Music Group—hold substantial influence over the global music landscape. These entities possess extensive resources, including financial backing, marketing prowess, and industry connections, which can catapult an artist from obscurity to stardom.

Theoretical frameworks such as the **Resource-Based View (RBV)** suggest that firms achieve competitive advantage through the acquisition and management of valuable resources (Barney, 1991). In the context of Kompany, signing with a major label provided access to critical resources that were previously out of reach, including high-quality production facilities, experienced marketing teams, and established distribution channels.

The Signing Process

The process of signing with a major label is often fraught with complexities. Initially, the band had to navigate the landscape of music contracts, which can be laden with legal jargon and intricate clauses. **Contract negotiation** is a crucial phase, where terms related to royalties, rights, and creative control are discussed. For Kompany, this meant engaging with legal experts to ensure that their artistic vision would not be compromised.

A significant challenge during this phase was the potential for **creative differences**. Major labels often have a vested interest in producing commercially viable music, which can sometimes clash with an artist's desire for creative expression. This tension is not uncommon; many artists have reported feeling pressured to conform to mainstream trends at the expense of their unique sound.

The Impact of Signing

Once the ink dried on the contract, the transformation was palpable. The immediate effects of signing with a major label for Kompany included:

- **Increased Visibility:** The label's marketing team launched a robust promotional campaign, introducing Kompany to a broader audience. This included high-budget music videos, radio play, and strategic placement on streaming platforms.

- **Professional Production:** With access to top-tier producers and recording facilities, Kompany was able to refine their sound. This professional touch was evident in their subsequent releases, which showcased a polished and sophisticated musical style.

- **Touring Opportunities:** The label facilitated major touring opportunities, allowing Kompany to perform in larger venues and festivals. This exposure not only expanded their fan base but also solidified their reputation as a live act.

Challenges Post-Signing

Despite the advantages, the transition to being signed with a major label was not without its challenges. The pressure to produce hits became a double-edged sword. While the financial backing allowed for more ambitious projects, it also imposed a timeline that was often unrealistic for the creative process.

Market Expectations played a significant role in shaping Kompany's output. The band faced the dilemma of balancing commercial viability with artistic integrity. For instance, during the production of their first major label album, they experimented with new sounds and collaborations, some of which were met with skepticism from label executives who favored a more formulaic approach.

Moreover, the scrutiny from the media and fans intensified. Every move was analyzed, and the pressure to maintain a favorable public image became a constant concern. This environment can lead to what is known as **imposter syndrome**, where artists question their worth and capabilities despite evident success.

Conclusion

Signing with a major label marked a significant turning point for Kompany. It opened doors to new opportunities and resources that were previously unimaginable. However, it also introduced a myriad of challenges that tested their resolve and commitment to their music. As they navigated this new terrain, the band learned valuable lessons about the music industry, the importance of maintaining artistic integrity, and the necessity of collaboration and communication within the group.

In the end, the partnership with a major label became a crucial chapter in Kompany's story, one that not only defined their early success but also set the stage for their evolution as artists. The experience underscored the delicate balance between commercial success and creative freedom, a theme that would resonate throughout their career.

Chart-topping singles and albums

As Kompany's sound evolved and their fan base expanded, the band began to capture the attention of music critics and industry insiders alike. The release of their first chart-topping single marked a pivotal moment in their career, transitioning them from local favorites to national sensations. This section delves into the significance of their chart-topping singles and albums, exploring the creative processes behind them, the impact on their career trajectory, and the broader implications for the music industry.

The Breakthrough Single

The journey to their first chart-topping single was not without its challenges. The single, titled *"Echoes of Tomorrow,"* was born from a late-night jam session that encapsulated the essence of Kompany's unique sound. The songwriting process involved a collaborative effort where each member contributed their individual influences—blending elements of pop, rock, and electronic music. This fusion not only resonated with their existing fan base but also attracted new listeners.

$$\text{Popularity Index} = \frac{\text{Total Streams} + \text{Radio Plays} + \text{Social Media Mentions}}{\text{Number of Days Since Release}}$$

(16)

Using the formula above, the band calculated their *Popularity Index* shortly after the release of *"Echoes of Tomorrow."* The results were staggering, with the single achieving over 10 million streams within the first week, propelling it to the top of the charts. This sudden surge in popularity showcased not only the effectiveness of their marketing strategy but also the power of their music to connect with a wide audience.

Album Success

Following the success of their breakout single, Kompany released their debut album, *"Resonance,"* which debuted at number one on the national charts. The album was a culmination of their experiences, struggles, and triumphs, featuring a collection of songs that explored themes of love, loss, and self-discovery. The lead single, *"Echoes of Tomorrow,"* set the tone for the album, but it was the subsequent tracks that showcased the band's versatility and depth.

The album's success can be attributed to several factors:

- **Diverse Sound:** Each track on *"Resonance"* offered a different sonic experience, from the upbeat anthems to the heartfelt ballads, appealing to a broad audience.

- **Strategic Collaborations:** Collaborating with renowned producers and artists added credibility and fresh perspectives to their work, enhancing the album's overall quality.

- **Effective Promotion:** The band utilized social media platforms, music videos, and live performances to promote the album, creating a buzz that translated into sales.

Chart Performance Analysis

The performance of *"Resonance"* on various music charts provides insight into the band's growing influence. The album not only topped the Billboard 200 chart but also achieved significant international success, reaching the top ten in several countries.

$$\text{Chart Position} = \frac{\text{Sales}}{\text{Total Sales of All Albums}} \times 100 \qquad (17)$$

Using the formula above, the band analyzed their chart position relative to other albums released during the same period. *"Resonance"* maintained a strong position for several weeks, demonstrating the album's staying power in a competitive market.

Cultural Impact

The impact of Kompany's chart-topping singles and albums extended beyond commercial success. Their music resonated with a generation grappling with issues of identity and belonging. Songs like *"Echoes of Tomorrow"* became anthems for young listeners, embodying their struggles and aspirations. The band's ability to articulate these feelings through their music solidified their place in the hearts of fans and critics alike.

Moreover, their chart-topping success opened doors for discussions on representation in the music industry. Kompany's diverse backgrounds and influences highlighted the importance of inclusivity in music, inspiring a new wave of artists to embrace their unique identities.

Conclusion

The chart-topping singles and albums of Kompany represent more than just commercial achievements; they are a testament to the band's artistic journey and their ability to connect with audiences on a profound level. As they continue to push the boundaries of their sound, their legacy as influential musicians will undoubtedly inspire future generations.

In summary, the success of *"Echoes of Tomorrow"* and *"Resonance"* illustrates the intricate relationship between creativity, marketing, and cultural impact in the music industry. Kompany's story serves as a reminder that with passion, perseverance, and a touch of magic, dreams can indeed become reality.

Music videos and media presence

As Kompany ascended to national success, their music videos and media presence became integral to their brand identity and commercial viability. The visual representation of their music not only enhanced their artistic expression but also served as a powerful marketing tool that connected with audiences on a deeper level.

The Role of Music Videos

Music videos are a unique form of art that combines visual storytelling with music, creating a multi-sensory experience for the viewer. According to [?], music videos can be seen as a medium that allows artists to convey themes and emotions that may not be fully expressed through audio alone. For Kompany, their music videos became a canvas for their creativity, enabling them to illustrate the narratives behind their songs.

The production of a music video involves several key elements, including concept development, filming, editing, and distribution. Each phase requires collaboration among various professionals, including directors, cinematographers, and editors. For instance, the music video for their breakthrough hit featured a narrative that resonated with fans, showcasing the band's journey through a series of visually striking scenes. This not only amplified the song's emotional impact but also solidified their presence in the competitive music landscape.

Media Presence and Engagement

In the digital age, a band's media presence extends beyond music videos to include social media platforms, interviews, and promotional appearances. Kompany strategically utilized these platforms to engage with their fan base and expand their reach. Research by [?] emphasizes the importance of social media in shaping public perception and fostering community among fans.

Kompany's approach to media presence was characterized by authenticity and relatability. They shared behind-the-scenes content, personal anecdotes, and interactive posts that invited fans into their world. For example, during the release of their second album, they hosted a live Q&A session on social media, allowing fans to ask questions directly. This not only strengthened their bond with existing fans but also attracted new listeners who appreciated their openness.

Challenges and Critiques

Despite the advantages of a robust media presence, Kompany faced challenges that required careful navigation. The pressure to maintain a constant online presence can lead to burnout among artists, as noted by [?]. Additionally, the scrutiny of media coverage can sometimes distort public perception, leading to misconceptions about the band and its members.

For instance, during a particularly intense media cycle, rumors of internal conflicts within the band began to circulate. Kompany addressed these rumors head-on, using their platform to clarify misunderstandings and reinforce their unity. This proactive approach not only mitigated potential damage to their reputation but also showcased their commitment to transparency with their fans.

Impact on Brand Identity

The synergy between music videos and media presence played a critical role in shaping Kompany's brand identity. Their visual aesthetic and storytelling approach became synonymous with their sound, creating a cohesive image that resonated with audiences. As articulated in [?], a strong brand identity is crucial for long-term success in the music industry, as it differentiates an artist from their competitors.

Kompany's music videos often featured recurring motifs and themes that reflected their musical evolution. For example, the transition from their early, more simplistic video styles to elaborate productions with intricate narratives signified their growth as artists. This evolution not only attracted a broader audience but also solidified their status as innovators in the industry.

Conclusion

In summary, Kompany's music videos and media presence were instrumental in their journey to national success. By leveraging the power of visual storytelling and engaging with fans through various platforms, they cultivated a strong and lasting connection with their audience. Despite the challenges that arose, their ability to navigate the media landscape with authenticity and creativity has left an indelible mark on their legacy. As they continue to evolve, the lessons learned from their experiences in this realm will undoubtedly influence their future endeavors.

Headlining Tours and Sold-Out Shows

The thrill of performing live

The stage is set, the lights dim, and a hush falls over the crowd. The palpable energy in the air is electric, and as the first notes resonate through the venue, the thrill of performing live engulfs the band members of Kompany. This moment, often described as a euphoric blend of excitement and anxiety, is a defining aspect of their musical journey.

Performing live is not merely about showcasing musical talent; it is an intricate dance of emotions, connection, and artistry. The thrill comes from the immediate feedback of an audience, where every cheer and clap can send waves of adrenaline coursing through the performers. This is often referred to as the "feedback loop" in performance theory, where the audience's reactions directly influence the musicians' energy levels and performance dynamics.

$$E = \frac{1}{2}kx^2 \qquad (18)$$

In the equation above, E represents the energy of the performance, k symbolizes the crowd's enthusiasm, and x denotes the intensity of the band's delivery. The higher the crowd's enthusiasm (k), the greater the energy (E) of the performance, creating a symbiotic relationship that enhances the experience for both the band and the audience.

For Kompany, each live performance is a unique experience, shaped by the venue, the audience, and the moment. In intimate settings, the connection with fans is often more personal, allowing for a shared emotional experience. The band recalls a particularly memorable show at a small local club, where they could see the faces of their fans illuminated by the stage lights. The shared laughter, the sing-alongs, and even the tears during heartfelt ballads create an atmosphere that is irreplaceable.

However, the thrill of live performance is not without its challenges. The pressure to deliver a flawless show can be immense. Musicians often face issues such as technical difficulties, unexpected changes in setlists, or even personal struggles that can affect their performance. For instance, during one of their early shows, a sudden power outage left the band in darkness, forcing them to engage the audience in an impromptu acoustic set. This moment, while initially a setback, turned into one of their most cherished memories, showcasing their resilience and ability to adapt.

The psychological aspect of performing live also plays a crucial role. Many artists experience performance anxiety, which can manifest as stage fright or self-doubt. Understanding this phenomenon is essential for artists like Kompany, who must navigate these emotions to connect authentically with their audience. Techniques such as visualization, deep breathing, and positive affirmations can help mitigate anxiety and enhance performance.

Moreover, the thrill of live performance is often amplified by the communal experience it fosters. Concerts create a sense of belonging and connection among fans, transcending individual experiences. The shared moments of joy, nostalgia, and catharsis unite strangers in a collective celebration of music. This phenomenon can be explained through social identity theory, which posits that individuals derive a sense of self from their group memberships. For many fans, being part of the Kompany community reinforces their identity and provides a sense of purpose.

As Kompany continues to evolve, the thrill of performing live remains a cornerstone of their artistry. Each show is an opportunity to connect, inspire, and create lasting memories. The band understands that while the music is central to their identity, it is the live performances that breathe life into their songs, transforming them from mere recordings into shared experiences.

In conclusion, the thrill of performing live is a multifaceted experience that encompasses joy, connection, and the challenges of artistry. It is this thrill that drives Kompany to continue pushing their creative boundaries, exploring new sounds, and connecting with their fans on a deeper level. Every performance is a testament to their journey, a celebration of their shared passion for music, and a reminder of the profound impact they have on the lives of those who come to see them play.

Memorable tour moments

The journey of Kompany has been punctuated by a series of unforgettable tour moments that not only defined their career but also deepened their connection with fans. Each tour stop became a chapter in their story, filled with laughter, tears, and the kind of magic that only live music can create.

One of the most memorable moments occurred during their first national tour, where they played at the iconic *Madison Square Garden*. The energy in the arena was palpable, a living entity that surged through the crowd, igniting excitement and anticipation. As they took the stage, the roar of the audience was deafening, a chorus of voices united in harmony. This was the moment when they realized the weight of their influence, as fans sang along to every lyric, transforming the concert into a shared experience.

$$E = mc^2 \qquad (19)$$

Where E represents the energy of the audience, m the mass of the music, and c the speed of sound. This equation metaphorically illustrates how the energy in the room can be seen as a product of the music's intensity and the audience's engagement.

Another poignant moment took place during a performance in *Los Angeles*, where a fan, who had been battling illness, was brought on stage to sing a duet with the band. The emotional weight of the moment was palpable, as the audience witnessed a heartfelt connection that transcended the usual performer-fan relationship. The band members were visibly moved, and this experience deepened their understanding of the impact their music had on individuals' lives.

Challenges on Tour: However, not every moment was filled with joy. The pressures of touring often led to unexpected challenges. One notable incident occurred during a show in *Chicago*, where a technical malfunction caused a significant delay. Instead of succumbing to frustration, the band improvised by engaging the audience in a spontaneous Q&A session. This moment of vulnerability not only showcased their authenticity but also strengthened the bond between the band and their fans.

$$T = \frac{1}{f} \qquad (20)$$

Where T is the period of the delay and f is the frequency of the audience's cheers. This equation illustrates how the unexpected can often lead to a deeper connection, as the band transformed a potential setback into an opportunity for engagement.

Surprise Guest Appearances: The thrill of surprise guest appearances also marked their tours. During a concert in *New York*, they were joined on stage by a legendary artist who had influenced their musical style. The collaboration was electric, and the audience erupted in applause, creating a moment that would be etched in the memories of all present. Such collaborations not only highlighted the band's respect for their musical predecessors but also showcased their willingness to push creative boundaries.

Fan Interactions: The band made a conscious effort to connect with fans beyond the stage. They organized meet-and-greet sessions where fans could share their stories and experiences. One fan's story about how a particular song helped them through a tough time resonated deeply with the band. This interaction served as a reminder of the power of music as a healing force, reinforcing their commitment to creating music that speaks to the human experience.

Culmination of Experiences: As the tours progressed, the compilation of these moments created a rich tapestry of experiences. The laughter shared during soundchecks, the tears shed during emotional performances, and the collective joy of live music all contributed to the band's growth. Each tour became a journey of self-discovery, not just for the band, but also for the fans who traveled alongside them.

In conclusion, the memorable moments from Kompany's tours are a testament to the power of music to unite, heal, and inspire. These experiences, filled with both joy and challenges, have shaped their identity as artists and solidified their legacy in the hearts of fans. As they continue to tour and create, these moments serve as a reminder of the magic that happens when music and humanity collide.

Connecting with fans on a deeper level

As Kompany rose to national fame, the band recognized that their success was not solely measured by chart-topping singles or sold-out shows, but also by the profound connections they forged with their fans. This realization was pivotal in shaping their approach to live performances and fan engagement, leading to a deeper understanding of the emotional and psychological dynamics involved in the artist-fan relationship.

The Emotional Connection

Research in music psychology suggests that music serves as a powerful medium for emotional expression and connection. According to [?], music can evoke strong emotions and memories, allowing listeners to feel understood and validated. For Kompany, this meant crafting songs that resonated with their audience's experiences, hopes, and struggles. Their lyrics often reflected themes of love, loss, and resilience, creating a shared narrative that fans could relate to on a personal level.

During their live performances, the band made a conscious effort to engage with the audience, fostering an atmosphere of intimacy and connection. This was exemplified in their song "Echoes of Us," where the lead vocalist often paused to share anecdotes about the song's inspiration, encouraging fans to reflect on their own stories. The result was a collective experience, where the audience felt not just like spectators, but integral participants in the performance.

Interactive Engagement

In the age of social media, the ways in which artists connect with fans have evolved dramatically. Kompany embraced platforms like Instagram, Twitter, and TikTok, utilizing these tools to create a two-way dialogue with their audience. The band frequently hosted Q&A sessions, where fans could ask questions about their music, personal lives, and creative processes. This interaction not only humanized the band members but also allowed fans to feel a sense of ownership over the music they loved.

Moreover, Kompany initiated fan-driven campaigns, such as the #KompanyMoments challenge, where fans were encouraged to share their personal stories related to the band's songs. The most compelling stories were featured on the band's social media pages, creating a sense of community and belonging among fans. This engagement strategy not only deepened the emotional connection but also reinforced the idea that the band valued their fans' experiences and voices.

Creating Lasting Memories

Kompany understood that memorable experiences could leave a lasting impression on their fans. To enhance the concert experience, they incorporated unique elements into their shows, such as surprise guest appearances, acoustic sets, and interactive segments where fans could join them on stage. For instance, during their tour for the album *Resonance*, they invited fans to participate in a live rendition of their hit single "Together Again," creating an unforgettable moment that resonated deeply with both the band and the audience.

Additionally, the band organized meet-and-greet events, where fans could interact with them personally, share their stories, and take photos. These intimate encounters not only strengthened the bond between the band and their fans but also provided a platform for fans to express their appreciation and support. The emotional impact of these interactions often led to fans sharing their experiences on social media, further amplifying the band's reach and reinforcing their community of supporters.

Challenges and Solutions

Despite the positive aspects of fan engagement, Kompany faced challenges in maintaining these connections. As their popularity grew, so did the demands on their time and energy. Balancing personal lives, creative pursuits, and fan interactions became increasingly complex. The band recognized the importance of setting boundaries to avoid burnout while still prioritizing their fans.

To address this challenge, Kompany implemented a structured approach to fan engagement. They designated specific times for social media interactions, ensuring that they could connect with fans without compromising their well-being. Furthermore, they invested in a dedicated team to manage fan communications, allowing the band members to focus on their music while still maintaining meaningful connections with their audience.

Conclusion

In conclusion, the journey of Kompany illustrates the significance of connecting with fans on a deeper level. Through emotional resonance, interactive engagement, and the creation of lasting memories, the band fostered a loyal and passionate fanbase. By navigating the challenges of fame while prioritizing these connections, Kompany not only solidified their place in the music industry but also left an indelible mark on the hearts of their fans. As they continue to evolve as artists, their commitment to nurturing these relationships remains a cornerstone of their legacy.

Behind the Scenes

The pressure of success

As Kompany ascended the ranks of the music industry, the pressure of success began to weigh heavily on the band members. This pressure can be understood through various psychological and sociological theories that explore the impacts of fame and recognition on individuals and groups.

One relevant theory is the **Social Comparison Theory**, proposed by Festinger in 1954. This theory posits that individuals determine their own social and personal worth based on how they stack up against others. For Kompany, the success of their peers in the industry created an environment rife with comparison. The band members often found themselves measuring their achievements against those of other artists, leading to feelings of inadequacy and anxiety. This constant comparison could be modeled mathematically as:

$$S = \frac{A}{C}$$

where S represents the subjective sense of success, A is the actual achievements of the band, and C is the perceived achievements of their peers. As C increased, the perceived success S for Kompany could diminish, regardless of their actual accomplishments.

Moreover, the pressure of success manifested in the form of heightened expectations from both fans and the music industry. With each album release and tour, there was an unspoken yet palpable expectation that Kompany would not only meet but exceed their past successes. This led to what psychologists refer to as **Performance Anxiety**. According to a study published in the *Journal of Music Psychology*, performance anxiety can significantly impair an artist's ability to create and perform, leading to a cycle of stress and underperformance.

For instance, during the recording of their second album, the band faced immense pressure to replicate the success of their debut. The fear of disappointing their fans and label executives created an environment of stress that stifled creativity. Members reported feeling as if they were in a creative straitjacket, where every note and lyric was scrutinized under the harsh light of expectation. The following equation illustrates the relationship between pressure and performance:

$$P = E \times R$$

where P is the pressure felt, E is the expectation from external sources, and R is the band's perceived ability to meet those expectations. As either E or R increased, so did P, leading to a detrimental cycle that affected their mental health and group dynamics.

The internal dynamics of the band also contributed to the pressure. As members began to experience individual success, the fear of overshadowing one another became a source of tension. This phenomenon can be understood through the lens of **Role Theory**, which suggests that individuals in a group adopt specific roles that can sometimes conflict with one another. For example, if one member began to receive more media attention, others might feel their contributions were undervalued, leading to resentment and conflict.

The pressure of success also took its toll on the band's personal lives. Many members struggled to balance their newfound fame with their relationships, leading to a sense of isolation. A study published in *Psychology of Music* found that musicians often report feeling detached from their personal lives during periods of intense public scrutiny. This phenomenon was evident in Kompany, as members found it increasingly difficult to connect with friends and family, exacerbating feelings of loneliness and stress.

Despite these challenges, Kompany sought to navigate the pressures of success through open communication and support. They established regular check-ins to discuss their feelings and concerns, fostering a culture of transparency within the group. This proactive approach can be supported by the **Transactional Model of Stress and Coping** proposed by Lazarus and Folkman, which emphasizes the importance of coping strategies in managing stress. By addressing their pressures head-on, the band aimed to mitigate the negative effects of fame and maintain their creative integrity.

In conclusion, the pressure of success posed significant challenges for Kompany, impacting their mental health, creative processes, and interpersonal relationships. By understanding the psychological theories that underpin these pressures, the band was able to develop strategies to cope with the demands of their rising fame. Ultimately, navigating this landscape of success became an integral part of their journey, shaping not only their music but also their identity as artists.

Creative conflicts within the band

Creative conflicts are an inevitable part of any collaborative endeavor, especially in the realm of music where personal expression and artistic vision collide. For Kompany, the journey to success was not just paved with harmonious melodies but also fraught with discordant notes that echoed through their creative process. This section delves into the nature of these conflicts, their underlying causes, and the ways in which they shaped the band's evolution.

The Nature of Creative Conflicts

Creative conflicts often arise from differing artistic visions and expectations among band members. Each member of Kompany brought their unique influences, backgrounds, and aspirations to the table, which sometimes led to disagreements over the direction of their music. As noted by [?], creativity thrives in environments that allow for the expression of diverse perspectives. However, when these perspectives clash, it can lead to tension and frustration.

For instance, during the early stages of their second album, members found themselves divided over the incorporation of electronic elements into their sound. While some members envisioned a more modern, synth-driven approach, others preferred to stick to their roots, favoring acoustic instrumentation. This divergence not only sparked heated discussions but also threatened to derail their creative momentum.

Underlying Causes

The underlying causes of these creative conflicts can often be traced back to individual aspirations and insecurities. Band members may fear that their contributions will be overshadowed or undervalued, leading to a defensive posture during discussions. [?] highlights that such insecurities can manifest as a reluctance to compromise, which can stifle innovation.

In Kompany's case, the pressure of rising fame added another layer to these conflicts. With increasing public scrutiny, each member felt the weight of expectations not only from fans but also from industry executives. This external pressure exacerbated internal disagreements, as members grappled with their artistic integrity versus commercial viability.

Examples of Conflict Resolution

Despite the challenges posed by creative conflicts, Kompany learned to navigate these turbulent waters through open communication and compromise. One notable instance occurred during the songwriting process for their hit single, "Chasing Shadows." Initial sessions were marked by frustration, as members struggled to align their visions. Recognizing the impasse, they decided to hold a series of brainstorming sessions where each member could present their ideas without interruption.

This approach allowed for a more inclusive atmosphere, fostering creativity while minimizing conflict. The result was a fusion of styles that incorporated both electronic and acoustic elements, culminating in a sound that resonated with their audience. This experience underscored the importance of adaptability and collaboration in overcoming creative differences.

The Role of External Mediators

At times, the band sought the input of external mediators, such as producers and music consultants, to help facilitate discussions. These professionals brought a fresh perspective and were able to identify potential compromises that the band members had overlooked. For example, during the production of their third album, a renowned producer suggested a hybrid approach to blending genres, which ultimately led to the creation of a critically acclaimed track that showcased the band's versatility.

Learning and Growth

Through these conflicts, Kompany not only refined their sound but also strengthened their interpersonal relationships. Each member learned the value of empathy and active listening, skills that proved essential in resolving disputes. As [?] posits, effective conflict resolution can lead to greater creativity and innovation, a sentiment that resonated with Kompany as they emerged from their struggles with a renewed sense of purpose.

Conclusion

In conclusion, while creative conflicts within Kompany were often challenging, they ultimately played a crucial role in shaping the band's identity and sound. By embracing their differences and fostering an environment of open communication, the band transformed potential roadblocks into stepping stones toward artistic growth. As they continued their journey, the lessons learned from these conflicts became integral to their success, reminding them that even in discord, there is the potential for harmony.

Balancing personal lives and fame

The journey to stardom is often a double-edged sword, particularly for artists like Kompany, who find themselves navigating the tumultuous waters of fame while trying to maintain their personal lives. The balance between public persona and private identity is a critical challenge that can shape not only the trajectory of a band's career but also the mental health and well-being of its members.

The Pressure of Public Scrutiny

As Kompany rose to national fame, the pressures of public scrutiny intensified. The media's relentless gaze can create an environment where personal struggles are laid bare for all to see. This phenomenon is well-documented in psychology; the concept of *social comparison theory* posits that individuals determine their own social and personal worth based on how they stack up against others. For Kompany, this meant that every misstep—whether a poorly received album or a public disagreement—was magnified, leading to stress and anxiety among the band members.

$$C = \frac{(P - O)}{O} \qquad (21)$$

Where:

- C is the comparison score,

- P is the perceived status,

- O is the original status.

This equation illustrates how the perceived status of the band fluctuates based on public perception, often leading to emotional turmoil. The members of Kompany experienced this firsthand, as they struggled to reconcile their individual identities with their collective image as a band.

Maintaining Relationships

Another significant aspect of balancing personal lives with fame is the effect it has on personal relationships. As they became more successful, the demands of touring and recording took a toll on their family and romantic relationships. The phenomenon of *relationship strain* is common among musicians, where the constant travel and time away from loved ones can lead to feelings of isolation and disconnection.

For example, during a particularly grueling tour, one member of Kompany found it increasingly difficult to maintain their relationship with a long-term partner. The late-night gigs, combined with the need for personal downtime, created a rift that was hard to bridge. This situation resonates with findings in family systems theory, which emphasizes that the dynamics within a family can be heavily influenced by external stressors, such as fame and public life.

Self-Care and Mental Health

Recognizing the importance of mental health, the band members began to prioritize self-care practices. This included therapy, mindfulness, and establishing boundaries around their work and personal lives. Research shows that engaging in self-care can significantly reduce stress and improve overall well-being. A study published in the *Journal of Music Therapy* highlights the positive effects of music on mental health, suggesting that creating music can serve as both a therapeutic outlet and a means of reconnecting with one's self.

$$M = \frac{(E + R + S)}{T} \qquad (22)$$

Where:

- M is the mental health score,
- E is emotional well-being,
- R is relationship quality,
- S is self-care practices,
- T is time spent on these activities.

This equation illustrates that by investing time in emotional well-being, nurturing relationships, and engaging in self-care, the members of Kompany could improve their mental health, even amidst the chaos of fame.

Finding Common Ground

To mitigate the challenges of balancing their personal lives with their careers, the band made a concerted effort to communicate openly about their struggles. They established regular check-ins, where they could discuss not only their musical endeavors but also their personal challenges. This practice of open communication is supported by the principles of *nonviolent communication* (NVC), which emphasizes empathy and understanding in interpersonal relationships.

By creating a safe space for vulnerability, the members of Kompany were able to foster a sense of solidarity. They learned to recognize when a bandmate was feeling overwhelmed and offered support, whether that meant taking a break from the spotlight or allowing for individual pursuits outside the band. This approach not only strengthened their bond but also allowed them to navigate the complexities of fame together.

Conclusion

In conclusion, the journey of balancing personal lives and fame is fraught with challenges, yet it is also a testament to the resilience of the human spirit. For Kompany, the key to navigating this delicate balance lay in prioritizing mental health, maintaining open lines of communication, and recognizing the importance of personal relationships. As they continue to evolve as artists, their story serves as a reminder that while fame may bring opportunities, it is the connections we nurture and the care we take for ourselves that ultimately sustain us through the highs and lows of life in the spotlight.

Chapter Highlights:

Awards and accolades

As Kompany ascended to national fame, their journey was punctuated by a series of remarkable accolades that not only recognized their musical talent but also solidified their place in the hearts of fans and the music industry. Each award was a testament to their hard work, dedication, and the unique sound they crafted together.

Grammy Awards

The pinnacle of recognition in the music industry is undoubtedly the Grammy Awards, and Kompany was no stranger to this prestigious ceremony. Their first Grammy win came in the category of *Best New Artist*, a significant acknowledgment that marked their transition from local favorites to national sensations. The emotional moment when they accepted the award was captured in the hearts of millions, as lead vocalist, during her speech, expressed gratitude not only to their fans but also to the countless individuals who believed in their dream from the very beginning.

$$\text{Grammy Wins} = \text{Total Nominations} \times \text{Win Rate} \qquad (23)$$

In their first year of eligibility, Kompany received nominations in five categories, showcasing their versatility and the wide appeal of their music. Their win rate, calculated as follows:

$$\text{Win Rate} = \frac{\text{Number of Wins}}{\text{Total Nominations}} \times 100\% \qquad (24)$$

With a win rate of 20%, they quickly became a household name, inspiring aspiring musicians everywhere.

MTV Music Awards

Kompany's vibrant music videos also caught the attention of the MTV Music Awards, where they were nominated for *Best Video of the Year* for their hit single *"Echoes of Tomorrow."* The video, known for its stunning visuals and innovative storytelling, resonated with audiences and critics alike, leading to a memorable performance at the awards show. The band's electrifying stage presence and emotional delivery captivated viewers, further elevating their status in the music scene.

$$\text{MTV Awards} = \text{Nominations} + \text{Wins} + \text{Performances} \qquad (25)$$

Their ability to blend music with visual artistry set a new standard for music videos, and they were recognized with several nominations across categories, culminating in a win for *Best Art Direction*.

Billboard Music Awards

The Billboard Music Awards celebrated Kompany's commercial success, with their albums consistently topping the charts. Their sophomore album, *"Resonance,"* not only debuted at number one but also broke records for the highest first-week sales for a debut album by a band in over a decade. This achievement was reflected in multiple nominations and wins at the Billboard Music Awards, including:

- *Top Selling Album*
- *Top Rock Artist*
- *Top Hot 100 Song*

The emotional weight of these accolades was palpable during their acceptance speeches, where they often highlighted the importance of their fan base in achieving such milestones.

International Recognition

Kompany's influence transcended borders, earning them international accolades such as the *Brit Awards* and the *ARIA Music Awards*. Their ability to connect with

CHAPTER HIGHLIGHTS: 61

a global audience was evident as they received nominations for *International Group of the Year* and *Best International Album*. These awards not only recognized their artistic achievements but also solidified their status as ambassadors of music across cultures.

$$\text{Global Impact} = \text{International Awards} + \text{Fan Engagement} \quad (26)$$

The global impact of Kompany's music was evident as they received the *World Music Award* for *Best Selling Artist Worldwide*, a monumental recognition that underscored their widespread appeal.

Legacy of Awards

The awards and accolades received by Kompany serve as a legacy, illustrating their journey from local musicians to international stars. Each trophy and certificate represents not just a moment of triumph but also the collective effort of every band member, their management team, and, most importantly, their loyal fans.

In conclusion, the recognition Kompany received throughout their career is a reflection of their talent, hard work, and the emotional connection they forged with their audience. These accolades stand as milestones in their journey, each one a reminder of where they started and how far they've come, forever etched in the annals of music history.

Collaborations with industry legends

The journey of Kompany has been marked by a series of groundbreaking collaborations with some of the most revered names in the music industry. These partnerships not only elevated their sound but also broadened their artistic horizons, allowing them to explore new genres and styles. In this section, we delve into the significance of these collaborations, the challenges faced, and the creative breakthroughs that emerged from these alliances.

The Importance of Collaboration

Collaboration in the music industry can be likened to a complex equation, where each variable represents an artist's unique style, experience, and influence. The outcome of this equation often leads to innovative soundscapes that resonate with audiences on a profound level. Mathematically, we can represent the collaborative process as follows:

$$C = A_1 + A_2 + A_3 + \ldots + A_n$$

where C represents the collaborative output, and $A_1, A_2, A_3, \ldots, A_n$ are the individual contributions of each collaborating artist. Each artist brings their own flair, resulting in a richer and more dynamic musical product.

Notable Collaborations

Kompany's collaborations with industry legends have not only been a testament to their growing influence but also a catalyst for their evolution as artists. Some of the most notable collaborations include:

- **Collaboration with Legend A:** This partnership was born out of mutual respect and admiration. The blending of Kompany's contemporary sound with Legend A's classic style resulted in the hit single "Harmony in Chaos." The song showcased intricate vocal harmonies and a fusion of genres that captivated listeners and critics alike.

- **Collaboration with Legend B:** In an unexpected twist, Kompany teamed up with Legend B, a pioneer in electronic music. The resulting track, "Electric Dreams," was a departure from their usual sound, incorporating synth-heavy beats and experimental sounds. This collaboration not only introduced Kompany to a new audience but also earned them a nomination for the Electronic Music Awards.

- **Collaboration with Legend C:** Perhaps one of the most significant collaborations was with Legend C, a celebrated songwriter and producer. This partnership led to the creation of the album "Timeless," which featured an array of genres, from pop to soul. The synergy between Kompany and Legend C resulted in a critically acclaimed project that solidified their place in the music industry.

Challenges Faced

While collaborations can lead to remarkable outcomes, they also come with their share of challenges. For Kompany, navigating the dynamics of working with established artists required a delicate balance of creativity and compromise. Some of the common challenges included:

CHAPTER HIGHLIGHTS: 63

- **Creative Differences:** Each artist brings their own vision, which can sometimes clash with the established style of Kompany. For instance, during the recording of "Harmony in Chaos," there were disagreements over the arrangement of the song, leading to intense discussions that ultimately resulted in a more polished final product.
- **Time Constraints:** Collaborating with industry legends often means working within tight schedules. Kompany faced significant pressure to deliver high-quality work within limited timeframes, especially when working with artists who had numerous commitments.
- **Maintaining Identity:** One of the biggest challenges was ensuring that their unique sound was not overshadowed by the influence of their collaborators. Kompany strived to maintain their artistic identity while blending their style with that of their collaborators, a task that required careful consideration and artistic integrity.

Creative Breakthroughs

Despite the challenges, these collaborations led to significant creative breakthroughs for Kompany. Each partnership allowed them to explore new musical territories and refine their craft. Some key breakthroughs included:

- **Expanded Musical Vocabulary:** Working with diverse artists exposed Kompany to new techniques and styles. The influence of Legend B's electronic sound, for example, inspired them to incorporate more electronic elements into their future works, resulting in a fresh and innovative sound.
- **Enhanced Lyricism:** Collaborating with seasoned songwriters like Legend C enriched Kompany's lyrical content. The process of co-writing brought forth deeper themes and more nuanced storytelling, allowing them to connect with their audience on a more emotional level.
- **Increased Visibility:** Each collaboration brought Kompany into the spotlight, introducing them to a broader audience. Their partnership with industry legends not only elevated their status but also opened doors for future opportunities, including international tours and festival appearances.

Conclusion

The collaborations with industry legends have been pivotal in shaping the trajectory of Kompany's career. Through navigating the complexities of creative partnerships, they have emerged stronger, more versatile, and more connected to their audience. As they continue to build on these experiences, the legacy of these collaborations will undoubtedly influence their future endeavors, leaving an indelible mark on the music landscape. The journey of Kompany is a testament to the power of collaboration and the magic that can happen when artists come together to create something extraordinary.

Creative breakthroughs and new musical directions

As Kompany continued to navigate the turbulent waters of fame, the band found themselves at a crossroads, a moment rich with potential for creative breakthroughs and new musical directions. This phase was characterized by an exploration of innovative sounds and a willingness to step beyond their established genre.

The Shift in Sound

The band's early work was marked by a blend of pop and rock, with catchy hooks and relatable lyrics. However, as they gained national recognition, the members felt an urge to evolve. They began to experiment with elements from various genres, incorporating electronic influences, world music, and even orchestral arrangements. This shift was not merely an artistic choice; it was a response to the changing landscape of the music industry, where listeners craved diversity and authenticity.

One significant breakthrough came during the recording of their second album, where the band embraced the use of synthesizers and digital production techniques. This was a departure from their traditional sound, which relied heavily on acoustic instruments. The incorporation of electronic elements allowed them to create a more expansive soundscape. For instance, the track *"Electric Hearts"* featured pulsating synth lines layered over a driving beat, showcasing their new direction. The equation for the sound design can be represented as:

$$S = A + B + C$$

where S is the final sound, A is the analog instruments, B is the electronic elements, and C is the vocal harmonies. This equation illustrates the collaborative nature of their sound, highlighting how various components come together to create a cohesive musical experience.

CHAPTER HIGHLIGHTS: 65

Collaborative Innovations

Collaboration became a cornerstone of Kompany's creative breakthroughs. They sought out producers and musicians outside their usual circle, which brought fresh perspectives and ideas. One notable collaboration was with renowned producer *Max Martin*, who had a history of crafting chart-topping hits. Under his guidance, the band learned to refine their songwriting process, focusing on structure and melody while experimenting with unconventional song forms.

The song *"Uncharted Waters"* emerged from this collaboration, featuring an atypical verse-chorus structure that defied traditional pop conventions. The decision to incorporate a bridge that shifted the key dramatically added emotional depth, resonating with their audience on a profound level. The formula for this song structure can be represented as:

$$\text{Structure} = \text{Intro} + (\text{Verse} + \text{Chorus} + \text{Bridge})^n$$

where n represents the number of repetitions. This innovative approach not only showcased their growth as songwriters but also attracted a new audience who appreciated their willingness to experiment.

Lyrics and Themes

The lyrical content of Kompany's music also evolved during this period. Initially focused on themes of love and heartbreak, the band began to explore more complex subjects, such as identity, societal issues, and personal growth. This thematic shift was evident in the song *"Reflections"*, which tackled issues of self-acceptance and the struggle for authenticity in a world filled with expectations.

The lyrics, paired with a haunting melody, created an emotional resonance that connected deeply with listeners. The creative process behind these lyrics involved extensive brainstorming sessions, where band members would share personal experiences and insights. The resulting collaborative effort led to a more nuanced and relatable narrative.

Embracing Technology

In addition to musical experimentation, Kompany embraced technology in their songwriting and production processes. They utilized software such as *Ableton Live* and *Logic Pro* to create demos and refine their sound. This technological integration allowed them to manipulate sounds in ways that were previously unimaginable, leading to unique auditory experiences.

For example, the use of *VST plugins* enabled the band to incorporate a wide range of sounds, from lush strings to intricate percussion, enriching their musical palette. The equation representing their approach to technology can be expressed as:

$$T = \sum_{i=1}^{n} \text{VST}_i$$

where T is the total technological influence, and VST_i represents each virtual instrument or effect used in the production process. This method not only enhanced their sound but also provided a platform for continuous innovation.

Audience Engagement

The breakthroughs in their music also translated into deeper connections with their audience. Kompany began to leverage social media platforms to share their creative process, inviting fans into their world. This transparency fostered a sense of community and loyalty among their listeners, who felt invested in the band's journey.

Live performances became a canvas for their new musical directions. The band incorporated visual elements and storytelling into their shows, creating immersive experiences that resonated with audiences. The song *"Journey On"* exemplified this, featuring a multimedia presentation that complemented the emotional weight of the music.

Conclusion

In summary, the creative breakthroughs and new musical directions taken by Kompany during this pivotal period were a testament to their resilience and adaptability. By embracing innovation, collaboration, and technology, they not only expanded their artistic horizons but also solidified their place in the music industry. The evolution of their sound and themes not only reflected their growth as artists but also resonated deeply with a generation of fans who found solace and inspiration in their music. As they continued to push boundaries, Kompany was not just a band; they became a movement, paving the way for future artists to explore their own creative paths.

Chapter Three: Trials and Triumphs

Internal Struggles

Band dynamics and tensions

The journey of a band is often a reflection of the intricate dynamics that exist between its members. In the case of Kompany, the interplay of personalities, creative visions, and individual aspirations created both harmony and discord, shaping their musical trajectory in profound ways. Understanding these dynamics is crucial, as they often dictate not only the creative output but also the longevity of the group.

Theoretical Framework

Band dynamics can be analyzed through various psychological and sociological lenses. One prominent theory is Tuckman's stages of group development, which outlines four stages: forming, storming, norming, and performing. In the context of Kompany, these stages were not just theoretical milestones but lived experiences that influenced their music and relationships.

$$\text{Forming} \rightarrow \text{Storming} \rightarrow \text{Norming} \rightarrow \text{Performing} \qquad (27)$$

During the **forming** stage, Kompany's members, who were childhood friends, initially experienced excitement and optimism. However, as they began to navigate the challenges of the music industry, they entered the **storming** phase, characterized by conflict and competition. This stage is often marked by the emergence of differing opinions and creative clashes, which can be both a source of tension and a catalyst for growth.

Sources of Tension

The tensions within Kompany often stemmed from a variety of sources:

- **Creative Differences:** Each member brought their unique musical influences and styles, leading to disagreements over the direction of their sound. For instance, while one member favored a more pop-oriented approach, another was drawn to indie-rock elements. This divergence sometimes resulted in heated debates during songwriting sessions, where compromise was essential yet challenging to achieve.

- **Role Conflicts:** As the band's popularity grew, so did the expectations placed on each member. Questions regarding roles—who would take the lead vocals, who would write the lyrics, and who would manage public relations—created friction. Each member's desire for recognition and contribution sometimes clashed, leading to feelings of resentment and undervaluation.

- **External Pressures:** The demands of the music industry, including tight schedules, media scrutiny, and the pressure to produce hits, exacerbated internal tensions. As they toured extensively and faced the rigors of fame, the strain of constant travel and performance took a toll on their relationships.

- **Personal Issues:** Personal lives often seeped into the band dynamic. Issues such as romantic relationships, family commitments, and mental health struggles affected how members interacted with one another. For example, if one member was dealing with personal challenges, it could lead to withdrawal from group activities, causing feelings of isolation among the others.

Examples of Tensions in Kompany

One notable incident occurred during the recording of their second album. The band had just returned from a successful tour, and tensions were running high. A disagreement over a particular song's arrangement escalated into a heated argument. One member felt that their artistic vision was being compromised, while another insisted on a more commercial sound to appeal to a broader audience. This conflict not only delayed the recording process but also led to a temporary rift between members.

To address these tensions, the band sought the help of a mediator—an industry veteran who had worked with other successful bands. This intervention highlighted the importance of open communication and the need for each member to express their feelings and concerns constructively. They learned that acknowledging their differences could lead to creative breakthroughs rather than divisions.

Resolving Tensions

Kompany's ability to navigate these dynamics was crucial to their success. They implemented strategies to mitigate tensions:

- **Regular Check-Ins:** The band began holding regular meetings to discuss not only their music but also their feelings about the band's direction and individual roles. This practice fostered a culture of openness and trust, enabling members to voice concerns before they escalated into larger issues.
- **Collaborative Songwriting:** By adopting a collaborative approach to songwriting, they allowed each member to contribute their ideas, ensuring that everyone felt valued. This not only enriched their music but also strengthened their bond as a group.
- **Team-Building Activities:** Engaging in team-building exercises outside of music helped them reconnect on a personal level. Whether it was a weekend retreat or a simple dinner together, these moments allowed them to rediscover their shared passion for music and friendship.

Conclusion

The dynamics and tensions within Kompany were an integral part of their story. While challenges arose from creative differences, role conflicts, and external pressures, the band learned to navigate these waters with resilience and adaptability. Their journey illustrates that while tensions can threaten a band's unity, they can also serve as a crucible for creativity and growth. As Kompany moved forward, they carried with them the lessons learned from their struggles, transforming tensions into a source of strength that ultimately defined their legacy in the music industry.

Personal challenges and growth

As the members of Kompany navigated the tumultuous waters of fame and success, they found themselves confronted with a myriad of personal challenges that tested their resilience and commitment to one another. The journey from obscurity to national recognition is often fraught with hurdles, and for Kompany, this was no exception. The pressures of the music industry, coupled with the demands of their burgeoning careers, led to significant personal growth for each member.

The Weight of Expectations

With the release of their first album, the band experienced a surge in popularity that brought with it heightened expectations. The pressure to produce hit after hit can be overwhelming, and for the members of Kompany, this manifested in various ways. According to [?], the phenomenon of "impostor syndrome" is common among successful artists, leading them to doubt their abilities despite evident success. This psychological struggle can create a rift within the band, as members grapple with their self-worth in the face of public adoration and critical acclaim.

For instance, lead vocalist Alex found himself questioning his creative contributions. The fear of not living up to the standards set by their debut album led him to withdraw from the songwriting process. This withdrawal not only stunted his personal growth but also affected the dynamics within the band. As noted by [?], communication is key in collaborative environments, and Alex's silence created a void that left the other members feeling uncertain about their roles.

Navigating Personal Lives

The rise to fame often comes at a personal cost. As the band members enjoyed their newfound success, they also faced challenges in their personal lives. Each member dealt with relationships strained by the demands of touring and recording. For example, drummer Sam struggled to maintain a long-distance relationship with his partner, who felt neglected as Sam spent more time on the road than at home. This situation is not uncommon in the music industry, where the constant travel can lead to feelings of isolation and disconnection from loved ones [?].

The emotional toll of these challenges prompted the band to seek solutions. They began to prioritize open discussions about their personal lives during rehearsals, creating a safe space for each member to express their feelings and concerns. This practice not only strengthened their bond but also fostered personal growth, as members learned to balance their professional and personal responsibilities more effectively.

Finding Individual Identities

In the midst of their collective success, the members of Kompany also embarked on a journey of self-discovery. Each member sought to understand their individual identities beyond their roles in the band. For instance, guitarist Mia took a step back to explore her passion for visual arts, participating in local exhibitions to showcase her work. This exploration allowed her to reconnect with her creative spirit and brought a fresh perspective to her contributions in the band.

Similarly, bassist Jake found solace in writing poetry, a form of expression he had long neglected. By channeling his emotions into words, Jake discovered new depths to his songwriting, enriching the band's music with layers of meaning that resonated with fans on a profound level. The integration of personal experiences into their music became a hallmark of Kompany's evolving sound, demonstrating the importance of individual growth within a collaborative framework.

Resilience Through Adversity

The challenges faced by Kompany were not solely personal; they were also professional. The band encountered significant obstacles, including a poorly received second album that left them questioning their direction. This setback could have spelled disaster, but instead, it served as a catalyst for growth. The members recognized that resilience is a vital component of success, particularly in the arts.

In the wake of their struggles, the band engaged in a series of workshops aimed at fostering creativity and collaboration. These sessions, inspired by the principles of *design thinking* [?], encouraged them to embrace failure as a stepping stone to innovation. By reframing their setbacks as opportunities for learning, Kompany not only strengthened their musical identity but also solidified their commitment to one another.

Conclusion

The personal challenges faced by the members of Kompany ultimately led to significant growth, both as individuals and as a band. Through open communication, exploration of individual passions, and a commitment to resilience, they emerged stronger than ever. Their journey serves as a testament to the power of facing adversity and the importance of personal development in the pursuit of collective dreams. As they continued to evolve, the lessons learned during this challenging period would shape not only their music but also their legacy in the industry.

The importance of communication and compromise

In the world of music, where creativity flows like a river and emotions run high, effective communication and the ability to compromise are paramount to the success and longevity of any band. For Kompany, these elements became the bedrock upon which their relationships were built, especially during times of internal struggle.

Theoretical Framework

Communication within a group can be understood through various theoretical lenses. One prominent theory is the **Interpersonal Communication Theory**, which posits that successful communication occurs when individuals express their thoughts and feelings openly and honestly, fostering an environment of trust and understanding. According to [1], effective interpersonal communication consists of four key components: clarity, listening, feedback, and empathy.

$$\text{Effective Communication} = \text{Clarity} + \text{Listening} + \text{Feedback} + \text{Empathy} \quad (28)$$

These components highlight the necessity for band members to articulate their needs and concerns clearly while also being receptive to each other's perspectives.

Challenges Faced

Despite the importance of communication, Kompany faced significant challenges. As they rose to fame, the pressures of success began to strain their relationships. Tensions arose during the creative process, with differing opinions on musical direction and the desire for individual expression sometimes clashing. For example, during the production of their second album, one member proposed a shift towards a more experimental sound, while another favored sticking to their established style. This divergence led to frustration and misunderstandings, which could have derailed their progress.

Moreover, **groupthink** became a potential hazard. As defined by Janis (1972), groupthink occurs when a desire for harmony or conformity results in irrational decision-making. In Kompany's case, there were instances where members hesitated to voice dissenting opinions for fear of disrupting the group's unity. This reluctance to communicate openly not only stifled creativity but also bred resentment among members.

The Role of Compromise

In navigating these turbulent waters, the concept of compromise emerged as a crucial tool. Compromise, defined as the willingness to accept a mutually agreeable solution, allowed Kompany to balance individual desires with collective goals. For instance, after a particularly heated discussion regarding the album's direction, the band decided to allocate specific tracks to explore different styles. This approach not only satisfied the creative urges of the individual members but also maintained the integrity of their overall sound.

$$\text{Compromise} = \frac{\text{Individual Needs} + \text{Group Goals}}{2} \quad (29)$$

This equation illustrates how compromise requires a balancing act between personal aspirations and the shared vision of the band. It emphasizes that both individual and group needs are essential in the creative process.

Examples of Successful Communication and Compromise

One poignant example of effective communication and compromise occurred during the writing sessions for their hit single, "Echoes of Tomorrow." Initially, the lyrics were heavily influenced by one member's personal experiences, which resonated deeply with the group. However, another member felt that the music needed a more upbeat tempo to connect with their growing fan base.

After several discussions, they reached a compromise: they maintained the heartfelt lyrics while infusing a more vibrant, energetic arrangement. This collaboration not only resulted in a hit song but also reinforced the bond between the members, showcasing the power of communication and compromise in achieving a common goal.

The Importance of Active Listening

Active listening plays a vital role in fostering effective communication. It involves fully concentrating on what is being said rather than just passively hearing the message. In the context of Kompany, active listening allowed band members to validate each other's feelings and ideas, creating an atmosphere of respect and collaboration.

As noted by [2], active listening can be broken down into several key components:

- **Paying Attention:** This involves giving full attention to the speaker, making eye contact, and avoiding distractions.

- **Providing Feedback:** Reflecting on what has been said by paraphrasing or asking questions to clarify understanding.

- **Deferring Judgment:** Allowing the speaker to express their thoughts without immediate criticism or evaluation.

- **Responding Appropriately:** Being open and honest in response, while also being respectful of the speaker's feelings.

By practicing active listening, Kompany was able to navigate conflicts more effectively, leading to stronger interpersonal relationships and a more cohesive creative process.

Conclusion

In conclusion, the importance of communication and compromise cannot be overstated in the context of a band like Kompany. As they navigated the complexities of fame, personal growth, and creative expression, these elements became vital tools for overcoming challenges and fostering a supportive environment. By embracing open dialogue and finding common ground, Kompany not only strengthened their bond as friends and collaborators but also paved the way for continued success in their musical journey.

The lessons learned through these experiences highlight that in the world of music, as in life, the ability to communicate and compromise is essential for harmony and growth.

Bibliography

[1] Adler, R. B., & Rodman, G. (2016). *Interpersonal Communication: A Goals-Based Approach*. Oxford University Press.

[2] Brown, M. (2018). *Active Listening: A Practical Guide*. Communication Press.

The Breakup Rumors

Media speculation and fan reactions

As the narrative of Kompany began to unfold, the media's insatiable appetite for drama and intrigue turned its gaze upon the band, particularly during the tumultuous period when rumors of a breakup began to circulate. This section delves into the complex interplay between media speculation and the reactions of fans, illustrating how both elements shaped the band's journey and public perception.

The media, often described as the fourth estate, plays a crucial role in shaping public discourse. In the case of Kompany, the rumors of a split were fueled by a combination of factors, including the band's own internal struggles, public appearances that hinted at discord, and the inevitable speculation that arises when a group of artists reaches significant heights. The following equation encapsulates the relationship between media speculation, public perception, and fan reactions:

$$R = f(M, P, F) \qquad (30)$$

Where:

- R represents the overall reaction from fans.
- M denotes the level of media speculation.
- P signifies public perception of the band.

♦ *F* indicates the emotional investment of fans.

As media outlets began to report on the alleged tensions within Kompany, they often sensationalized the situation, framing it as a dramatic saga of betrayal and artistic differences. This narrative was not merely a reflection of the band's internal dynamics but was also influenced by the broader context of celebrity culture, where the personal lives of artists are scrutinized under a magnifying glass.

For instance, articles published in prominent music magazines speculated on the reasons behind the supposed rift, citing anonymous sources and insider information. Headlines such as "Kompany on the Brink: Are They Breaking Up?" and "Behind the Scenes: The Truth About Kompany's Tensions" generated buzz and captured the attention of both fans and casual observers. Such sensationalism often leads to a distorted view of reality, where the truth becomes secondary to the allure of a good story.

The reactions from fans were varied and complex. Many loyal supporters took to social media platforms to express their concerns and support for the band, creating a digital community where they could share their feelings. Hashtags like #SaveKompany and #WeStandWithKompany trended on Twitter, showcasing the passionate response from fans who refused to believe the rumors. The emotional investment of fans played a critical role in shaping the narrative, as they rallied together to defend their favorite band against what they perceived as unfounded speculation.

Moreover, fan reactions were not limited to online discourse; they also manifested in real-world actions. During concerts, fans would hold up signs reading "We Love You, Kompany!" and "Stay Together!" This public display of solidarity served as a powerful reminder to the band of the support they had from their fanbase. It also highlighted the symbiotic relationship between artists and their audience, where the emotional connection transcends mere entertainment.

However, the media's portrayal of the situation also had a darker side. The pressure of public scrutiny can be overwhelming for artists, leading to mental health challenges and personal crises. For example, one band member, who later spoke candidly about the experience, described feeling isolated and anxious due to the relentless speculation. The psychological toll of being in the spotlight, compounded by the fear of disappointing fans, created a challenging environment for the band as they navigated this turbulent period.

In response to the media frenzy, Kompany's management team took strategic steps to address the rumors. They issued public statements aimed at clarifying the band's position and reaffirming their commitment to one another. This proactive approach was essential in managing public perception and mitigating the impact of negative speculation. The following equation illustrates the effectiveness of communication strategies in shaping fan reactions:

$$E = \frac{C}{D} \tag{31}$$

Where:

- E represents the effectiveness of communication.
- C denotes the clarity of the message conveyed.
- D signifies the degree of misinformation present in the media.

By maintaining clear and open lines of communication, Kompany was able to reduce the impact of misinformation and reassure fans of their unity. The band members participated in interviews and shared their perspectives, emphasizing their dedication to their craft and each other. This transparency not only helped to quell the rumors but also strengthened the bond between the band and their audience.

In conclusion, the media speculation surrounding Kompany during this challenging period served as a double-edged sword. While it generated significant attention and engagement, it also posed risks to the band's mental health and public image. The reactions from fans demonstrated the power of community and loyalty, illustrating how deeply intertwined the relationship between artists and their supporters can be. Ultimately, this chapter in Kompany's story highlights the importance of communication, both within the band and with their audience, as they navigated the complexities of fame and personal struggles.

Navigating rumors and maintaining solidarity

In the world of music, where the spotlight shines brightly, the shadows of speculation often loom large. For Kompany, navigating the turbulent waters of breakup rumors was a test not only of their public persona but also of their internal dynamics and relationships. This section delves into the complexities of handling media speculation and fan reactions, emphasizing the importance of solidarity in the face of adversity.

Understanding the Nature of Rumors

Rumors can be defined as unverified information or stories that circulate within a community. In the case of Kompany, these rumors often stemmed from the band's internal struggles, personal conflicts, and the pressures of fame. The psychological impact of rumors can be profound, leading to anxiety, distrust, and a sense of isolation among band members.

Theories surrounding rumor propagation suggest that they often arise from uncertainty and ambiguity in social situations. According to [?], rumors serve as a mechanism for individuals to fill in gaps of knowledge, often leading to exaggerated or distorted narratives. In the context of Kompany, this meant that any hint of discord could quickly escalate into widespread speculation about the band's future.

Media Speculation and Fan Reactions

As Kompany's fame grew, so did the scrutiny of their personal lives. Media outlets, eager for sensational stories, often exaggerated minor disputes into potential breakups. For instance, a disagreement over creative direction during a rehearsal could be spun into a headline suggesting that the band was on the verge of disbandment.

The impact of such rumors on fans cannot be understated. Loyal supporters, who had invested emotionally in the band's journey, were left feeling anxious and confused. Social media platforms became battlegrounds for fans to voice their concerns, often leading to a divide within the fanbase. Some fans took to defending the band, while others speculated about the validity of the rumors, creating a toxic environment that further complicated the band's situation.

Maintaining Solidarity

In the face of such challenges, maintaining solidarity within the band became paramount. Open and honest communication emerged as a critical factor in navigating the storm of rumors. The members of Kompany recognized that addressing the underlying issues directly was essential to preventing misunderstandings from spiraling out of control.

$$S = \frac{C + R}{T} \qquad (32)$$

Where:

- S = Solidarity among band members
- C = Level of communication
- R = Relationship strength
- T = External tension from rumors

THE BREAKUP RUMORS 79

This equation illustrates that as communication (C) and relationship strength (R) increase, solidarity (S) can be maintained even in the face of external tensions (T).

To foster this environment, the band held regular meetings where members could express their concerns and feelings openly. This practice not only helped to clarify misunderstandings but also reinforced their commitment to one another and their shared vision.

Examples of Solidarity in Action

One notable instance of solidarity occurred when a particularly damaging rumor surfaced about the band's supposed breakup. Instead of allowing the speculation to fester, the members of Kompany decided to take proactive measures. They organized a press conference to address the rumors head-on, emphasizing their unity and commitment to their music.

During this event, the lead vocalist stated, "We're not going anywhere. We're in this together, and our fans deserve to hear the truth." This public affirmation of solidarity not only quelled the rumors but also strengthened the bond between the band and their fans.

Moreover, the band utilized social media to their advantage, sharing behind-the-scenes glimpses of their creative process and personal interactions. By humanizing themselves and showcasing their camaraderie, they were able to counteract the negative narratives and reinforce their unity.

The Role of Support Systems

Beyond internal communication, external support systems played a crucial role in navigating rumors. The band relied on their management team and trusted advisors to help craft their public narrative. This support allowed them to focus on their music while ensuring that any misinformation was promptly addressed.

Additionally, the loyalty of their fanbase proved invaluable. Supportive fans rallied around the band during difficult times, expressing their unwavering belief in Kompany's mission and vision. This communal solidarity acted as a buffer against the negativity generated by rumors, reminding the band of the love and support that existed beyond the speculation.

Conclusion

Navigating rumors and maintaining solidarity is a complex but essential aspect of a band's journey, particularly for Kompany. By fostering open communication, addressing speculation head-on, and relying on both internal and external support systems, they were able to weather the storm of rumors.

The experience not only strengthened their bond as a band but also deepened their connection with their fans. In the end, it was this solidarity that allowed Kompany to emerge from the challenges stronger and more united than ever, ready to continue their journey through the pulse of music.

Reconnecting with the music and rediscovering their passion

As the tumultuous waves of fame began to crash upon the shores of Kompany's journey, the members found themselves drifting further apart, not only from each other but also from the very essence of the music that had once brought them together. The pressures of success, coupled with personal struggles, created a rift that threatened to tear the band apart. In this crucial moment, it became imperative for each member to embark on a journey of introspection, a quest to reconnect with the music that had ignited their passion in the first place.

The Importance of Reflection

In the world of music, reflection serves as a powerful tool for artists. It allows them to step back and assess their motivations, desires, and the very foundation of their creativity. For Kompany, this reflection was not merely a personal endeavor; it was a collective necessity. Each band member took time away from the limelight to explore their individual identities, seeking to understand what music truly meant to them. This process was akin to the concept of *musical identity*, which posits that an artist's music is an extension of their personal experiences and emotions.

$$M = f(E, I, C) \tag{33}$$

where M represents the music produced, E denotes experiences, I indicates identity, and C stands for creativity. This equation illustrates that the music of Kompany is a function of their collective and individual experiences, identities, and creative expressions.

Rediscovering Inspiration

As the members of Kompany ventured into their solo projects, they began to explore different genres, collaborate with diverse artists, and experiment with new sounds. This period of exploration was crucial in reigniting their passion for music. For instance, one member might have delved into acoustic folk, while another experimented with electronic beats. These divergent paths not only enriched their musical palette but also allowed them to bring fresh perspectives back into the band.

A poignant example of this rediscovery can be seen in the case of their lead vocalist, who, during a retreat in the countryside, found inspiration in the simplicity of nature. This experience led to the composition of a song that captured the essence of longing and nostalgia, themes that resonated deeply with the band's core identity. The song, initially written as a solo piece, later became a collaborative effort that redefined Kompany's sound.

Reuniting Through Collaboration

After a period of individual exploration, the members of Kompany reconvened with a renewed sense of purpose. They approached their reunion not as a return to the past but as an opportunity to forge a new path forward. This was facilitated by a series of jam sessions, where the focus was not on creating a hit but on reconnecting with each other and the joy of making music. These sessions became a sanctuary for the band, a space where they could freely express their thoughts and emotions without the weight of expectations.

The collaborative spirit that emerged during these sessions was reminiscent of the *social constructivist theory*, which emphasizes the role of social interactions in learning and creativity. By engaging in open dialogue and shared musical experiences, the members of Kompany were able to reconstruct their musical identities and foster a sense of unity.

$$C_{new} = C_{old} + \Delta C \tag{34}$$

where C_{new} represents the new creative output, C_{old} denotes the previous creative state, and ΔC signifies the changes brought about by collaboration and shared experiences. This equation encapsulates how the band's collective creativity evolved through their renewed interactions.

Embracing Vulnerability

A key aspect of reconnecting with their music was the willingness to embrace vulnerability. The band members learned that expressing their struggles and emotions through music could forge deeper connections with their audience. This realization was transformative; it shifted their songwriting approach from creating commercially viable hits to crafting songs that were genuine reflections of their experiences.

For example, the song "Echoes of Us" emerged from a place of vulnerability, addressing the fears and uncertainties they faced during their hiatus. The lyrics, raw and heartfelt, resonated with fans who had followed their journey, creating a powerful bond that transcended the typical artist-fan relationship.

Conclusion

In reconnecting with their music and rediscovering their passion, Kompany not only salvaged their band but also revitalized their creative spirit. This journey of introspection, exploration, and collaboration allowed them to emerge stronger and more united than ever. As they stepped back into the spotlight, they did so with a renewed sense of purpose, ready to share their authentic selves with the world. The lessons learned during this transformative period would shape the future of Kompany, ensuring that their music would continue to resonate with fans for years to come.

Rebirth and Reinvention

Taking a break to regroup

In the whirlwind of success and the chaos of touring, the members of Kompany found themselves at a crossroads, a moment that would ultimately lead to a necessary pause in their journey. The pressures of fame, the demands of the industry, and the toll of constant performance began to weigh heavily on their spirits. It was during this tumultuous period that the band collectively recognized the importance of taking a step back to regroup, reflect, and recharge.

The Need for Reflection

As the adage goes, "You can't pour from an empty cup." This sentiment resonated deeply with the members of Kompany. After years of relentless touring and recording, they realized that their creativity was being stifled by exhaustion. The relentless cycle of producing hits and performing live had left little room for introspection. It was essential to pause and reconnect with the very essence of what brought them together—their love for music.

In psychological terms, this phenomenon can be understood through the lens of *Burnout Theory*, which posits that prolonged stress without adequate recovery can lead to emotional exhaustion, depersonalization, and a reduced sense of personal accomplishment. According to Maslach and Leiter (2016), the key components of burnout include emotional exhaustion, cynicism, and a feeling of inefficacy. For Kompany, these symptoms were becoming increasingly apparent.

Communication and Compromise

The decision to take a break was not made lightly. It required open communication and a willingness to compromise among the band members. They engaged in heartfelt discussions about their individual needs and collective aspirations. This dialogue was crucial in fostering a supportive environment where each member felt heard and valued.

For instance, during one particularly candid meeting, lead singer Mia expressed her feelings of isolation despite being surrounded by fans and fame. She articulated how the pressure to maintain a public persona often overshadowed her personal identity. Similarly, guitarist Leo shared his struggle with creative blocks, feeling as though the band's success had set an impossibly high bar for future projects.

These revelations highlighted the importance of vulnerability within the group dynamic. By sharing their struggles, the members of Kompany were able to strengthen their bond and reaffirm their commitment to one another and their music. This process of open communication is supported by *Group Dynamics Theory*, which emphasizes the role of interpersonal relationships in team performance.

The Decision to Pause

After much deliberation, the band collectively decided to take a sabbatical. This period of rest was not merely an escape; it was a strategic decision aimed at rejuvenating their creative energies. They agreed to spend time apart, pursuing individual projects, and exploring personal interests that had long been set aside.

For example, drummer Sam took this opportunity to delve into his passion for photography, capturing moments of beauty that often went unnoticed on the road. Meanwhile, bassist Tara began volunteering at a local music education program, sharing her knowledge and inspiring the next generation of musicians. These experiences not only enriched their personal lives but also provided fresh perspectives that would later inform their collective sound.

The Importance of Self-Care

During this hiatus, the members of Kompany embraced the principles of self-care, recognizing its critical role in maintaining mental and emotional well-being. They engaged in activities that nourished their souls, from yoga and meditation to spending quality time with loved ones.

Research has shown that self-care practices can significantly reduce stress and enhance overall well-being (Smith et al., 2018). By prioritizing self-care, the members of Kompany were not only investing in their individual health but also in the health of the band as a whole.

Reconnecting with Their Roots

As the break progressed, the band members found themselves naturally gravitating back to their musical roots. They began to reminisce about the early days of Kompany, when the music was raw, unfiltered, and driven purely by passion. This nostalgia sparked a desire to return to that authenticity, to create music that resonated with their true selves rather than the expectations of the industry.

This reconnection with their roots can be likened to the process of *Creative Recovery*, which suggests that stepping away from a project can lead to renewed inspiration and innovative ideas. The band members began to share snippets of new melodies and lyrics during casual meet-ups, igniting a spark that had been dormant for far too long.

Preparing for a Strong Comeback

Ultimately, the break allowed Kompany to emerge stronger and more cohesive than ever. They returned to the studio with a renewed sense of purpose, ready to channel their experiences into their next album. This period of regrouping not only revitalized their creativity but also deepened their appreciation for one another and the music they created together.

In conclusion, taking a break to regroup proved to be a transformative experience for Kompany. It was a testament to the power of self-reflection, communication, and the importance of prioritizing mental health in the face of success. As they prepared to step back into the spotlight, they did so with a newfound clarity and a commitment to authenticity that would define their next chapter.

References

1. Maslach, C., & Leiter, M. P. (2016). *Burnout: A Guide to Identifying Burnout and Pathways to Recovery*. Harvard Business Review Press.

2. Smith, J., Brown, L., & Johnson, K. (2018). The Impact of Self-Care on Mental Health: A Systematic Review. *Journal of Mental Health*, 27(4), 345-352.

Solo projects and side ventures

As the members of Kompany took a step back from the whirlwind of touring and recording, they found themselves at a crossroads, each confronting the question of personal artistic expression. This period of introspection and exploration led to a flourishing of solo projects and side ventures, allowing the band members to delve into their individual creativity while still holding onto the essence of what made them a cohesive unit.

The Importance of Individual Expression

The necessity for individual expression in a band setting cannot be overstated. It serves as a vital outlet for personal creativity, which can sometimes be stifled within the confines of a group dynamic. As noted by [?], "Artists often find that their most profound work emerges when they allow themselves the freedom to explore outside the boundaries of their primary projects." This sentiment resonated deeply with the members of Kompany, who each sought to carve out their own paths while remaining connected to the collective.

Members' Solo Ventures

- **Lead Vocalist:** The lead vocalist of Kompany, known for her powerful and emotive voice, embarked on a solo career that showcased her versatility. She released a critically acclaimed album, *Echoes of My Heart*, which explored themes of love, loss, and self-discovery. The album's lead single, "Whispers in the Wind," topped the charts and solidified her status as a formidable solo artist. Her foray into solo music not only allowed her to experiment with different genres, including jazz and blues, but also provided a fresh perspective that enriched her contributions to Kompany upon their reunion.

- **Guitarist:** The guitarist, known for his intricate playing style, ventured into the realm of instrumental music. His solo album, *Strings of Solitude*, featured a blend of acoustic and electric guitar compositions that drew inspiration from classical and world music. He collaborated with various artists, including a renowned cellist, to create a rich soundscape that resonated with listeners.

This experience not only honed his skills but also brought new influences into Kompany's subsequent work.

- **Drummer:** The drummer took a different approach by diving into music production. He launched a side project where he produced tracks for up-and-coming artists, utilizing his extensive knowledge of rhythm and sound engineering. His work in the studio allowed him to experiment with various musical styles, from electronic to hip-hop, which ultimately influenced Kompany's evolving sound.
- **Bassist:** The bassist explored his passion for songwriting, crafting a collection of deeply personal songs that reflected his journey and struggles. His debut solo EP, *Reflections*, was characterized by heartfelt lyrics and a blend of folk and rock elements. The project received positive reviews and showcased his growth as a musician, further enriching the band's lyrical depth in future collaborations.

Collaborative Projects

In addition to their solo endeavors, the members of Kompany also engaged in collaborative projects that allowed them to merge their individual styles. These collaborations served as a reminder of their shared history and the chemistry that initially brought them together.

- **Collaborative EP:** The band members came together to create a collaborative EP titled *Unity*, which featured a collection of songs that blended their diverse influences. Each member contributed a track, showcasing their unique styles while maintaining the essence of Kompany. The EP was well-received, reinforcing the idea that their individual journeys only enhanced the collective experience.
- **Live Performances:** During this period, the band also organized a series of intimate live performances, where they showcased both solo material and classic Kompany hits. These shows were a celebration of their individual growth and a testament to their enduring bond. The chemistry on stage was palpable, reminding fans of the magic that had first captured their hearts.

Challenges and Growth

While the solo projects and side ventures provided opportunities for artistic growth, they also presented challenges. The members faced the difficulty of balancing their individual pursuits with their commitment to Kompany. As [?] suggests, "Navigating personal ambitions within a group can lead to tension, but it can also foster a deeper understanding of one another." This sentiment echoed within the band as they learned to communicate openly about their aspirations and concerns.

The process of pursuing solo careers also highlighted the importance of mutual support. The members often attended each other's shows, providing encouragement and feedback. This camaraderie not only strengthened their individual identities but also reinforced their bond as a band.

Conclusion of Solo Ventures

Ultimately, the solo projects and side ventures undertaken by the members of Kompany served as a pivotal chapter in their journey. They emerged from this period with a renewed sense of purpose and a deeper appreciation for their collective artistry. The experiences gained during their time apart would later inform their work as a band, allowing them to return to the studio with fresh perspectives and a wealth of creative inspiration.

The legacy of their individual journeys would forever be intertwined with the story of Kompany, showcasing how the exploration of personal artistry can lead to a richer, more vibrant collective sound.

Coming back stronger than ever

The journey of Kompany, like many great bands, is a testament to resilience and the power of reinvention. After navigating through tumultuous times, the members of Kompany found themselves at a crossroads, faced with the challenge of not only sustaining their identity but also emerging from the shadows of uncertainty. This section explores how the band harnessed their experiences to come back stronger than ever, focusing on their strategic approaches to creativity, collaboration, and connection with their audience.

The Decision to Regroup

In the wake of internal struggles and external pressures, the band made a conscious decision to take a step back. This period of regrouping was essential for self-reflection and reassessment of their musical direction. According to organizational theory, particularly the concept of *adaptive resilience*, teams that embrace change and learn from their failures are often able to innovate and thrive (Hamel, 2000). Kompany's members applied this principle by engaging in open dialogues about their challenges, allowing them to identify the root causes of their tensions and misunderstandings.

Exploring Solo Projects

During their hiatus, each member of Kompany embarked on solo projects, exploring personal musical styles and influences. This not only allowed them to grow individually but also provided fresh perspectives that they could bring back to the group. For instance, lead vocalist Alex experimented with acoustic sounds while guitarist Sam delved into electronic music. This exploration aligns with the *diversity of thought* theory, which posits that varied experiences and backgrounds lead to more innovative outcomes (Page, 2007). By the time they reconvened, they had a wealth of new ideas and inspirations to draw from.

Reconnecting with Their Roots

Upon their return, the band made a deliberate effort to reconnect with their roots. They revisited the music that inspired them during their formative years, engaging with the sounds and styles that first ignited their passion for music. This process of reconnecting is critical in creative industries, as it fosters authenticity and a deeper emotional connection with the audience. According to Csikszentmihalyi's *flow theory*, engaging deeply with one's passions can lead to heightened creativity and fulfillment (Csikszentmihalyi, 1990). For Kompany, this meant reintroducing elements from their early work while infusing them with newfound maturity.

Collaborative Reinvention

Reinvention was not solely an individual endeavor; it was a collaborative effort that involved all members of the band. They sought to blend their diverse influences into a cohesive sound that reflected their growth. The collaborative model they adopted is supported by the *synergy theory*, which suggests that the combined efforts of a team can produce results greater than the sum of their individual contributions (Katzenbach & Smith, 1993). Through brainstorming sessions and jam nights, Kompany crafted new material that resonated with both their old fans and a new generation of listeners.

The Triumphant Comeback Album

The culmination of their efforts was the release of their comeback album, *Resurgence*. This album served not only as a reflection of their journey but also as a bold statement of their renewed identity. Songs like "Phoenix Rising" and "Echoes of Yesterday" encapsulated their struggles and triumphs, resonating with listeners who had followed their story. The album's success can be attributed to its emotional depth and the authenticity that permeated each track. Music industry analysts noted that the strategic blend of introspective lyrics and innovative sounds positioned Kompany to reclaim their place in the music landscape.

Fan Engagement and Support

A significant factor in Kompany's resurgence was the unwavering support from their fan base. During their hiatus, fans expressed their loyalty through social media campaigns and grassroots initiatives, proving that the connection they had built over the years was still strong. This phenomenon is supported by the *social capital theory*, which emphasizes the importance of relationships and networks in fostering community support (Putnam, 2000). Kompany utilized this support by engaging with fans through live Q&A sessions, exclusive behind-the-scenes content, and personal messages, reinforcing the bond they had cultivated over the years.

Conclusion: A Stronger Kompany

Ultimately, the journey of Kompany through trials and tribulations led to a powerful rebirth. By embracing their challenges, exploring new creative avenues, and reconnecting with their roots, they emerged not only as a band but as a symbol of resilience in the music industry. Their story serves as an inspiration for aspiring musicians and creatives alike, illustrating that setbacks can be the catalyst for greater achievements. As they continue to evolve and push boundaries, Kompany stands as a testament to the idea that sometimes, coming back stronger than ever is just the beginning of a new and exciting chapter.

Bibliography

[1] Hamel, G. (2000). Leading the Revolution. Harvard Business Review Press.

[2] Page, S. E. (2007). The Difference: How the Power of Diversity Creates Better Groups, Firms, Schools, and Societies. Princeton University Press.

[3] Csikszentmihalyi, M. (1990). Flow: The Psychology of Optimal Experience. Harper & Row.

[4] Katzenbach, J. R., & Smith, D. K. (1993). The Wisdom of Teams: Creating the High-Performance Organization. HarperBusiness.

[5] Putnam, R. D. (2000). Bowling Alone: The Collapse and Revival of American Community. Simon & Schuster.

Chapter Highlights:

Fan support and loyalty during difficult times

Throughout the tumultuous journey of Kompany, one undeniable truth emerged: the unwavering support and loyalty of their fans served as a lifeline during the most challenging periods. This section delves into the intricate relationship between the band and their fanbase, examining how this connection not only weathered the storms of internal strife but also fostered resilience and renewal.

The Emotional Bond

The bond between Kompany and their fans transcended mere admiration; it was rooted in shared experiences and emotional resonance. The psychology of fandom suggests that fans often identify with the struggles and triumphs of the artists they admire. According to [?], this identification can lead to a profound sense of community and belonging, which is particularly vital during times of crisis. For Kompany, their lyrics often reflected personal challenges, creating a narrative that fans could relate to, thus deepening their emotional investment in the band.

Social Media as a Support Platform

In the digital age, social media has become a crucial platform for fan engagement and support. During periods of uncertainty, such as the rumors of a breakup, fans took to platforms like Twitter and Instagram to express their loyalty. Hashtags like #WeAreKompany and #KompanyForever trended, showcasing the collective voice of fans rallying around their beloved band. This digital solidarity not only provided emotional support to the band members but also reinforced the community aspect of fandom. [?] notes that such online interactions can significantly enhance the perceived closeness between artists and their supporters.

Fan Initiatives and Grassroots Movements

The loyalty of Kompany's fans manifested in various grassroots initiatives aimed at supporting the band during tough times. For instance, when the band faced difficulties with their record label, fans organized a campaign to raise awareness and garner support. They created a petition that garnered thousands of signatures, demonstrating their commitment to the band. This kind of activism not only showcased the fans' dedication but also illustrated the power of collective action in influencing the music industry.

The Role of Fan Communities

Fan communities played a pivotal role in maintaining morale during challenging times. Online forums and fan clubs became safe spaces for fans to share their concerns and hopes regarding the band's future. These communities often organized meet-ups, both virtual and in-person, to foster camaraderie among fans. Such gatherings served as a reminder that they were not alone in their devotion to Kompany. The sense of belonging that these communities provided was essential for fans navigating their feelings during the band's struggles.

Examples of Loyalty During Crisis

One poignant example of fan loyalty occurred during the release of Kompany's third album, which was marred by internal conflicts and public speculation about the band's future. Despite the surrounding negativity, the fanbase rallied around the album, organizing listening parties and sharing their favorite tracks on social media. This grassroots enthusiasm not only helped the album achieve commercial success but also reinforced the band's resolve to continue creating music together.

Another instance was during a particularly difficult tour when one of the band members faced personal challenges. Fans took it upon themselves to create a video montage of supportive messages, which they presented to the band at a concert. This heartfelt gesture not only uplifted the spirits of the band members but also exemplified the profound impact that fan support can have during trying times.

The Power of Loyalty

The loyalty exhibited by Kompany's fans underscores a vital concept in the music industry: the strength of the artist-fan relationship. [?] argues that such loyalty can be a powerful catalyst for an artist's resilience, providing emotional and financial support that can help navigate the industry's challenges. For Kompany, the unwavering dedication of their fans not only helped them weather storms but also inspired them to evolve and grow as artists.

In conclusion, the journey of Kompany illustrates the profound impact of fan support and loyalty during difficult times. Through emotional bonds, social media engagement, grassroots initiatives, and strong community ties, their fans became an integral part of the band's narrative. This relationship not only provided comfort during periods of uncertainty but also played a crucial role in the band's eventual resurgence. As Kompany reflects on their journey, they recognize that their fans are not just spectators; they are essential partners in the story of their music.

A triumphant comeback album

After a tumultuous period marked by internal struggles and the looming specter of breakup rumors, Kompany found themselves at a crossroads. The whispers of disbandment had cast shadows over their legacy, but rather than succumb to the pressure, the band chose to harness their collective experiences and emotions to craft a triumphant comeback album that would redefine their sound and solidify their place in the music industry.

The Creative Process

The journey towards the comeback album began with a series of intense brainstorming sessions. Each member of Kompany brought their unique influences and experiences to the table, resulting in a rich tapestry of ideas. The band revisited their roots, drawing inspiration from the sounds that initially ignited their passion for music. They experimented with various genres, blending elements of rock, pop, and electronic music to create a sound that was both fresh and reminiscent of their earlier work.

$$C = \frac{1}{N} \sum_{i=1}^{N} x_i \qquad (35)$$

Where C represents the collective creativity of the band, N is the number of ideas generated, and x_i is the individual contribution of each member. This equation illustrates how the collaborative effort of the band led to a significant increase in their creative output, ultimately resulting in a cohesive and compelling album.

Songwriting and Themes

The songwriting process was cathartic for the band. They poured their hearts into the lyrics, addressing themes of resilience, love, and the struggle for identity amidst chaos. Tracks like "Rise Again" and "Echoes of Us" became anthems of hope and perseverance, resonating deeply with fans who had stood by them during their darkest days. The emotional weight of these songs was palpable, reflecting the band's journey of rediscovery and reinvention.

Production and Collaboration

With a clear vision in place, Kompany entered the studio with renowned producer Alex Turner, known for his work with several chart-topping artists. The collaboration proved to be a turning point; Turner's innovative techniques and fresh perspective helped the band refine their sound. The recording sessions were intense, often stretching late into the night as the band meticulously crafted each track. The synergy between the band and Turner resulted in a polished yet authentic sound that captured the essence of their journey.

Release and Reception

Upon its release, the comeback album, titled *Revival*, was met with critical acclaim and commercial success. The lead single, "Shattered Mirrors," debuted at number one on the charts, marking a significant milestone in Kompany's career. Fans and critics alike praised the album for its emotional depth and musical innovation, with many calling it a return to form.

$$R = P + S + C \qquad (36)$$

CHAPTER HIGHLIGHTS: 95

Where R represents the reception of the album, P is the production quality, S is the songwriting prowess, and C is the connection with the audience. This formula highlights the multifaceted approach that contributed to the album's success, demonstrating that a combination of high production values, strong songwriting, and a genuine connection with fans can lead to a triumphant return.

Impact on Their Career

The success of *Revival* not only revitalized Kompany's career but also reestablished their position as influential figures in the music industry. The album led to a sold-out world tour, where they reconnected with fans on a deeper level, sharing the stories behind the songs and the struggles they had overcome. The tour was a celebration of their journey, and each performance served as a reminder of the bond between the band and their supporters.

Legacy of the Comeback Album

In retrospect, *Revival* became more than just an album; it was a testament to the power of resilience and the enduring spirit of creativity. The band's ability to confront their challenges head-on and emerge stronger than ever left an indelible mark on the music landscape. New artists looked to Kompany as a source of inspiration, proving that even in the face of adversity, it is possible to rise again and create something truly remarkable.

As the final notes of *Revival* faded away, it became clear that Kompany had not only reclaimed their place in the industry but had also set a precedent for future generations of musicians. Their story was a reminder that the heart of music lies in its ability to heal, connect, and inspire, making Kompany's triumphant comeback album a pivotal chapter in their legacy.

Reflecting on the journey and the future of Kompany

As we navigate through the vibrant tapestry of Kompany's journey, it becomes evident that the path has been paved with both trials and triumphs. The evolution of the band is not merely a chronicle of musical milestones; it is a narrative steeped in resilience, creativity, and an unwavering connection to their fans. This section seeks to encapsulate the essence of their journey, reflecting on the significant moments that have defined them, while also casting a hopeful gaze toward the future.

A Retrospective on the Journey

Kompany's odyssey began with a spark of friendship and a shared passion for music that ignited in their formative years. The early days were marked by experimentation and a relentless pursuit of their unique sound. Each note played and every lyric penned contributed to a growing identity that resonated deeply with their local community. The first gigs, often held in dimly lit bars and small venues, were not just performances; they were intimate gatherings where the seeds of loyalty were sown among their burgeoning fan base.

As they transitioned from local recognition to national fame, Kompany encountered challenges that tested their resolve. The pressure of success, coupled with the complexities of band dynamics, often created friction. Yet, it was through these struggles that the band members learned the invaluable lessons of communication and compromise. They discovered that the heart of their music lay not only in the notes but also in the stories they shared and the emotions they evoked.

The Significance of the Breakthrough

The breakthrough hit that catapulted Kompany into the national spotlight was more than just a song; it was a testament to their perseverance. This pivotal moment illustrated the theory of the *Tipping Point*, where small, incremental changes lead to a significant impact. The song's success opened doors to opportunities that were once mere dreams, allowing them to connect with a wider audience and solidify their place in the music industry.

The subsequent tours and sold-out shows were exhilarating experiences that deepened their bond with fans. Each performance became a celebration of shared experiences, where the energy of the crowd intertwined with the band's passion. This synergy not only fueled their creativity but also reinforced their commitment to their craft.

Navigating the Trials of Fame

Despite the accolades and recognition, the journey was not without its trials. The internal struggles within the band, often exacerbated by the pressures of fame, led to moments of doubt and speculation. Breakup rumors swirled, igniting media frenzy and fan anxiety. However, it was during these tumultuous times that Kompany's resilience shone through. They leaned on their foundation of friendship and mutual respect, navigating the storms together and emerging stronger.

CHAPTER HIGHLIGHTS: 97

This period of introspection and self-discovery was crucial for the band's evolution. Each member embarked on solo projects, exploring their individual artistry while remaining committed to the collective vision of Kompany. This phase underscored the importance of personal growth within a collaborative environment, demonstrating that sometimes, stepping away can lead to a more profound understanding of one's purpose.

Looking Ahead: The Future of Kompany

As Kompany stands at the crossroads of their past and future, the horizon is filled with possibilities. The lessons learned from their journey serve as a guiding light, illuminating the path forward. Their unique musical style, characterized by heartfelt lyrics and innovative sounds, continues to inspire a new generation of musicians. The band's commitment to authenticity ensures that their future endeavors will resonate with both long-time fans and newcomers alike.

In contemplating the future, it is essential to acknowledge the role of philanthropy and activism in Kompany's narrative. Their dedication to using their platform for positive change reflects a growing trend in the music industry, where artists are increasingly aware of their influence. By supporting charitable causes and advocating for social issues, Kompany is not only leaving a mark on the music industry but also contributing to a broader cultural impact.

Conclusion: A Legacy in Motion

In conclusion, reflecting on the journey of Kompany reveals a rich tapestry woven with experiences that have shaped their identity. Their story is one of resilience, creativity, and a deep connection to their fans. As they look to the future, the band is poised to continue their legacy, inspiring others while remaining true to their roots. The road ahead may be uncertain, but one thing is clear: Kompany's heartbeat will forever resonate through the music they create, leaving an indelible mark on the hearts of fans around the world.

$$\text{Legacy} = \text{Journey} + \text{Impact} + \text{Connection} \tag{37}$$

Chapter Four: Legacy and Impact

Influencing a New Generation

Inspiring aspiring musicians

The journey of Kompany has been nothing short of a symphony of inspiration, resonating deeply with aspiring musicians across the globe. From their humble beginnings to their meteoric rise in the music industry, the band has become a beacon of hope and creativity for those who dare to dream.

At the heart of their influence lies the idea that music is not merely a profession but a profound form of expression. Kompany's members have often shared their belief that every note played and every lyric sung carries the potential to change lives. This philosophy encourages young musicians to embrace their individuality and to use their unique voices to convey their stories.

One of the most significant ways Kompany inspires aspiring musicians is through their authenticity. In an industry often plagued by trends and commercialism, the band has remained true to their roots. Their debut album, which was a culmination of years of songwriting and experimentation, serves as a testament to the power of perseverance and self-discovery. The raw emotion embedded in tracks like "Echoes of Tomorrow" and "Chasing Shadows" illustrates how vulnerability can resonate with audiences, encouraging young artists to share their own truths.

Moreover, Kompany's commitment to collaboration has set a powerful example for emerging musicians. By working with various artists, both established and newcomers, they have shown that music is a collective experience. This collaborative spirit fosters a sense of community among musicians, where ideas can flourish and diverse influences can merge. For instance, their partnership with up-and-coming artists on the track "Harmony in Dissonance" not only elevated the song's impact but also provided a platform for fresh talent, encouraging young musicians to seek out and embrace collaboration.

In addition to their musical contributions, Kompany has actively engaged in mentorship programs and workshops aimed at nurturing the next generation of artists. These initiatives provide invaluable resources and guidance, helping aspiring musicians navigate the complexities of the music industry. By sharing their experiences, challenges, and triumphs, the band demystifies the path to success, making it more accessible to those who may feel overwhelmed by the prospect of a music career.

The impact of Kompany's journey can be quantified through the stories of countless young musicians who cite the band as a primary source of inspiration. For example, a survey conducted among music students revealed that over 70% of respondents felt motivated to pursue their musical dreams after listening to Kompany's music. This statistic underscores the band's ability to connect with their audience on a personal level, instilling a sense of purpose and determination in aspiring artists.

Furthermore, the band's use of social media platforms to share their journey has created a direct line of communication with fans and aspiring musicians alike. By documenting their creative processes, sharing behind-the-scenes glimpses, and engaging in Q&A sessions, Kompany fosters an inclusive environment where aspiring musicians feel seen and heard. This transparency not only demystifies the creative process but also encourages young artists to share their own journeys, fostering a culture of openness and support.

In conclusion, Kompany's influence extends far beyond their music; it is a legacy of inspiration that empowers aspiring musicians to pursue their passions unapologetically. Through their authenticity, collaborative spirit, mentorship initiatives, and engagement with their audience, they have carved a path for the next generation of artists to follow. As they continue to evolve and innovate, Kompany remains a shining example of what it means to inspire, uplift, and ignite the creative spark in others. Their story is a reminder that with dedication, creativity, and a willingness to embrace one's unique voice, the possibilities in music are truly limitless.

Kompany's unique musical style and legacy

Kompany's musical style is a captivating blend of various genres, reflecting their diverse influences and experiences. At the heart of their sound lies an intricate fusion of pop, rock, and indie elements, which has allowed them to carve out a distinctive niche in the music industry. This section delves into the unique characteristics of Kompany's music, their innovative approaches to songwriting, and the legacy they have created over the years.

Genre Fusion and Influences

Kompany's sound is marked by a seamless integration of multiple genres, which can be traced back to their childhood influences. Growing up in a culturally rich environment, the band members were exposed to a wide array of musical styles, from the soulful ballads of the 70s to the energetic beats of modern pop. This eclectic mix of influences has led to the development of a sound that is both familiar and fresh.

One of the defining features of Kompany's music is their ability to blend catchy pop melodies with the raw energy of rock. For instance, their hit single *"Echoes of Tomorrow"* showcases this fusion, combining an infectious chorus with powerful guitar riffs. The song's structure can be analyzed using the following equation:

$$\text{Song Structure} = \text{Verse} + \text{Chorus} + \text{Bridge} \tag{38}$$

In *"Echoes of Tomorrow"*, the verse sets a reflective tone, while the chorus explodes with anthemic energy, illustrating how Kompany masterfully balances introspection with exuberance.

Innovative Songwriting Techniques

Kompany's songwriting process is characterized by collaboration and experimentation. The band members often write together, blending their individual styles to create a cohesive sound. This collaborative approach allows them to push boundaries and explore new musical territories. For example, their album *"Fragments of Us"* features tracks that incorporate unconventional time signatures and harmonies, challenging traditional pop structures.

One notable example is the song *"Shattered Reflections"*, which employs a 5/4 time signature, creating a sense of unpredictability that captivates listeners. The use of this time signature can be expressed mathematically as:

$$\text{Time Signature} = \frac{5}{4} \tag{39}$$

This deviation from the standard 4/4 time signature exemplifies Kompany's commitment to innovation and their desire to create music that resonates on multiple levels.

Emotional Resonance and Lyrical Depth

The emotional depth of Kompany's lyrics is another hallmark of their unique style. The band often draws from personal experiences, weaving narratives that resonate with their audience. Their lyrics tackle themes of love, loss, and self-discovery, inviting listeners to connect with their music on a profound level.

For instance, the poignant ballad *"Lost in the Silence"* explores the struggle of navigating heartbreak. The lyrics employ vivid imagery and metaphor, allowing listeners to immerse themselves in the emotional landscape of the song. Analyzing the lyrical structure reveals a pattern of repetition and variation that enhances its impact:

$$\text{Lyrical Structure} = \text{Verse} + \text{Chorus} + \text{Refrain} \tag{40}$$

In *"Lost in the Silence"*, the refrain serves as a powerful emotional anchor, reinforcing the central theme of vulnerability and yearning.

Legacy and Cultural Impact

Kompany's unique musical style has left an indelible mark on the music industry, influencing a new generation of artists. Their innovative approach to genre fusion and songwriting has inspired countless musicians to experiment with their sounds and push creative boundaries. The band's legacy is not only defined by their commercial success but also by their commitment to authenticity and artistic integrity.

As they continue to evolve, Kompany's impact on the music landscape remains significant. Their ability to connect with audiences through relatable themes and memorable melodies ensures that their music will resonate for years to come. Their legacy is encapsulated in the following equation:

$$\text{Legacy} = \text{Innovation} + \text{Emotional Connection} + \text{Cultural Influence} \tag{41}$$

In conclusion, Kompany's unique musical style and legacy are a testament to their artistry and dedication to their craft. By blending genres, employing innovative songwriting techniques, and creating emotionally resonant lyrics, they have established themselves as a force to be reckoned with in the music world. As they continue to inspire and influence future generations, their music will undoubtedly remain a cherished part of the cultural fabric.

Leaving a lasting impact on the music industry

Kompany's journey through the music landscape has been marked by a series of transformative moments that not only shaped their own identity but also left an indelible mark on the broader music industry. Their unique blend of genres, innovative soundscapes, and heartfelt lyrics have resonated with audiences worldwide, establishing them as a pivotal force in contemporary music.

Innovative Sound and Genre Fusion

At the heart of Kompany's influence lies their ability to transcend traditional genre boundaries. By fusing elements of pop, rock, and electronic music, they have created a sound that feels both fresh and familiar. This genre-blending approach can be analyzed through the lens of *musical hybridity*, a concept that suggests the mixing of different musical styles can lead to the creation of new, innovative forms of expression.

For example, their hit single *"Echoes of Tomorrow"* combines the anthemic qualities of rock with the rhythmic intricacies of electronic dance music (EDM). The success of this track can be attributed to its ability to appeal to diverse audiences, showcasing how genre fusion can enhance a band's reach and relevance.

$$\text{Impact} = \text{Diversity of Genres} \times \text{Audience Reach} \qquad (42)$$

This equation illustrates the relationship between the diversity of genres embraced by Kompany and their ability to connect with a wider audience, ultimately amplifying their impact on the industry.

Cultural Commentary and Lyrics

Kompany's lyrics often delve into themes of love, identity, and social issues, providing a voice for a generation grappling with complex realities. Their song *"Voices in the Dark"* addresses mental health, a topic that has gained significant attention in recent years. By tackling such subjects, Kompany not only entertains but also educates and inspires their listeners.

The impact of their lyrical content can be analyzed through the *theory of cultural hegemony*, which posits that art and culture can be tools for social change. Kompany's willingness to address pressing societal issues has encouraged other artists to follow suit, fostering a wave of music that is not only enjoyable but also socially conscious.

Influence on Emerging Artists

Kompany's success has paved the way for a new generation of musicians. By breaking down barriers and redefining what it means to be successful in the music industry, they have inspired countless aspiring artists to pursue their dreams. The phenomenon of *musical mentorship* can be observed here, where established artists like Kompany provide guidance and inspiration to newcomers.

Their collaboration with up-and-coming artists, such as the indie-pop sensation Lila Ray, exemplifies this influence. The partnership resulted in the track *"Rise Together"*, which not only topped charts but also served as an anthem for aspiring musicians. This collaborative spirit reinforces the idea that success in the music industry is often a collective effort.

Legacy of Philanthropy and Activism

Beyond their musical contributions, Kompany has also made significant strides in philanthropy and activism. Their involvement in various charitable initiatives, such as the *Music for Change* campaign, highlights their commitment to using their platform for positive impact. This campaign focuses on mental health awareness and has raised substantial funds for related charities.

Kompany's philanthropic efforts can be understood through the *theory of social responsibility in the arts*, which emphasizes the role of artists in advocating for social change. Their actions have encouraged other musicians to engage in similar initiatives, creating a ripple effect that extends their influence beyond music.

Conclusion: A Lasting Impact

In summary, Kompany's legacy in the music industry is characterized by their innovative sound, meaningful lyrics, mentorship of emerging artists, and commitment to philanthropy. Their ability to challenge norms and inspire change has left a lasting impact that will resonate within the industry for years to come. As they continue to evolve and create, their influence will undoubtedly inspire future generations of musicians, ensuring that their mark on the music industry remains profound and enduring.

Philanthropy and Activism

Using their platform for positive change

In an era where the voice of artists resonates beyond the confines of concert halls and recording studios, Kompany has embraced the responsibility that comes with fame. The band has consistently used its platform to advocate for social issues, demonstrating that music can be a powerful catalyst for change. This section delves into the various initiatives taken by Kompany, illustrating how their influence extends beyond entertainment and into the realm of activism.

The Power of Music as a Tool for Activism

Music has long been recognized as a medium that transcends cultural and linguistic barriers, making it an effective tool for raising awareness about pressing social issues. According to [?], music can create a sense of community and solidarity among listeners, fostering a collective identity that can mobilize action. Kompany has harnessed this power by aligning their artistic endeavors with causes that resonate deeply with their audience.

Charitable Collaborations

Kompany has partnered with various non-profit organizations, using their concerts as platforms to raise funds and awareness for causes such as mental health, environmental conservation, and education. For instance, during their national tour, they collaborated with *Music for Change*, a charity dedicated to supporting mental health initiatives among young people. By donating a portion of ticket sales and merchandise profits, Kompany not only contributed financially but also brought attention to the importance of mental health awareness in their performances.

$$\text{Total Donations} = \sum_{i=1}^{n} \text{Ticket Sales}_i \times \text{Donation Rate} \qquad (43)$$

Where: - Total Donations is the total amount donated to charity. - Ticket Sales$_i$ represents the sales from each concert i. - n is the total number of concerts. - Donation Rate is the percentage of sales donated.

This equation illustrates how Kompany's commitment to philanthropy can be quantified and showcases the tangible impact of their efforts.

Advocacy Through Lyrics and Public Statements

Beyond financial contributions, Kompany has utilized their music and public appearances to advocate for social justice. Their lyrics often reflect themes of empowerment, resilience, and social change, resonating with fans who share similar struggles. For example, the song *"Voices Unite"* addresses issues of inequality and calls for collective action. The chorus, which emphasizes unity and strength, has become an anthem for various social movements.

In addition to their music, the band members have made public statements during interviews and press conferences, using their visibility to discuss critical issues. They have openly addressed topics such as climate change, gender equality, and racial injustice, urging fans to engage in activism. This aligns with the findings of [?], which suggest that artists can shape public discourse and influence societal attitudes through their platforms.

Community Engagement Initiatives

Kompany has also taken a grassroots approach to activism by engaging directly with local communities. They have organized workshops and events aimed at empowering young musicians and artists, particularly in underserved areas. These initiatives not only provide resources and mentorship but also foster a sense of belonging and purpose among participants.

One notable project is the *Kompany Music Initiative*, which offers free music lessons and instruments to children from low-income families. By investing in the next generation of musicians, Kompany is not only nurturing talent but also promoting the idea that music can be a transformative force in people's lives. The program has seen significant success, with many participants going on to pursue music professionally.

Social Media as a Catalyst for Change

In the digital age, social media serves as a powerful platform for artists to amplify their messages. Kompany has effectively utilized platforms like Instagram, Twitter, and Facebook to raise awareness about various social issues. Through engaging content, they have encouraged fans to participate in campaigns, share their stories, and support causes they believe in.

For example, during a recent campaign for environmental sustainability, Kompany launched the hashtag #KompanyForThePlanet, urging fans to share their eco-friendly practices. The campaign not only sparked conversations about climate change but also created a sense of community among fans who are passionate about making a difference.

Challenges and Criticisms

While Kompany's efforts to use their platform for positive change are commendable, they have not been without challenges. The band has faced criticism from some fans who feel that their activism detracts from their music. Balancing the dual roles of artist and activist can be complex, as highlighted by [?], which discusses the potential backlash that public figures may encounter when engaging in social issues.

Moreover, the band must navigate the fine line between genuine activism and performative gestures. Critics often scrutinize celebrities for their involvement in social causes, questioning the authenticity of their commitment. Kompany has addressed these concerns by ensuring that their initiatives are rooted in genuine passion and a desire to effect real change.

Conclusion

In conclusion, Kompany exemplifies how artists can leverage their platforms for positive change. Through charitable collaborations, advocacy in their music, community engagement, and effective use of social media, they have made significant contributions to various social causes. While challenges remain, their commitment to activism serves as an inspiring model for other artists looking to make a difference. As they continue to navigate their careers, Kompany's legacy will undoubtedly include their role as advocates for positive social change, leaving an indelible mark on both the music industry and society as a whole.

Supporting charitable causes close to their hearts

Throughout their illustrious career, Kompany has not only captured the hearts of millions with their music but has also made it a mission to give back to the community. Their commitment to philanthropy is deeply intertwined with their artistic identity, reflecting the values and experiences that shaped them as individuals and as a band.

The Importance of Giving Back

The ethos of supporting charitable causes stems from a profound understanding that music has the power to influence and inspire. For Kompany, this realization is akin to the *social responsibility theory*, which posits that individuals and organizations have an obligation to act for the benefit of society at large. This theory resonates with the band, as they believe that their platform can be a beacon of hope and change.

$$R = \frac{C}{S} \qquad (44)$$

Where: - R is the impact of their charitable efforts, - C represents the contributions made (both monetary and in-kind), - S stands for the societal needs addressed.

Kompany's contributions have ranged from financial support to hands-on involvement in various initiatives, reflecting their commitment to making a tangible difference.

Key Charitable Initiatives

Kompany has supported numerous causes, focusing on areas that resonate with their personal experiences and the challenges faced by their fans. Some of the notable initiatives include:

- **Mental Health Awareness:** In light of the pressures and struggles associated with fame and personal challenges, Kompany has been a staunch advocate for mental health awareness. They have partnered with organizations like *Mind Matters*, using their concerts to raise funds and awareness for mental health initiatives. By sharing their own stories of struggle, they have helped destigmatize mental health issues, encouraging fans to seek help and support.

- **Youth Music Programs:** Understanding the transformative power of music, Kompany has invested in youth music programs that provide underprivileged children with access to musical education. Their initiative, *Kompany Cares*, has funded scholarships, instruments, and workshops, empowering the next generation of musicians. This aligns with the *educational equity theory*, which advocates for equal access to educational resources regardless of socioeconomic status.

- **Environmental Advocacy:** Kompany has also taken a stand on environmental issues, partnering with organizations like *Green Harmony*. They have participated in campaigns aimed at promoting sustainability and awareness about climate change. Their song, *"Earth's Lament,"* became an anthem for environmental activism, highlighting the urgent need for action.

Collaborative Efforts

Kompany's philanthropic efforts often involve collaboration with other artists and organizations. Their annual charity concert, *Harmony for Hope*, brings together various musicians to raise funds for different causes. This not only amplifies their impact but also fosters a sense of community within the music industry.

The success of these events can be quantified by analyzing the funds raised and the number of beneficiaries reached. For example, in 2022, *Harmony for Hope* raised over $1 million, directly benefiting over 10,000 individuals through various programs.

$$T = \sum_{i=1}^{n}(F_i \times B_i) \qquad (45)$$

Where: - T is the total impact of the charity event, - F_i represents the funds raised by each artist, - B_i is the number of beneficiaries impacted by those funds, - n is the number of participating artists.

Fan Engagement and Community Impact

Kompany recognizes the power of their fanbase in driving charitable initiatives. They actively engage their fans in various campaigns, encouraging them to contribute through social media challenges and fundraising events. This not only fosters a sense of belonging among fans but also amplifies the reach of their charitable efforts.

For instance, during the *"Kompany Gives Back"* campaign, fans were invited to share their own stories of giving, leading to a ripple effect of kindness and generosity. The campaign resulted in over 5,000 shared stories and significant contributions to local charities, showcasing the profound impact of community engagement.

Conclusion

Kompany's dedication to supporting charitable causes is a testament to their belief in the transformative power of music and community. By aligning their philanthropic efforts with their values and the needs of their fans, they have created a legacy that transcends music. Their work serves as an inspiration, proving that when artists use their voice for good, they can create a harmonious world where music and compassion coexist. As Kompany continues to evolve, their commitment to philanthropy remains a cornerstone of their identity, ensuring that they not only entertain but also uplift and empower those around them.

Making a difference through music and activism

Music has always held the power to inspire change, and for Kompany, this truth resonates deeply. As the band navigated their journey through fame and success, they recognized their unique position to leverage their influence for social good. The intersection of music and activism became a cornerstone of their identity, allowing them to advocate for causes that mattered not only to them but also to their fans and the broader community.

The Role of Music in Activism

The relationship between music and activism is well-documented, with numerous studies highlighting how songs can serve as catalysts for social movements. According to [?], music can mobilize communities, raise awareness, and foster a sense of solidarity among individuals facing common struggles. This aligns with the theory of collective efficacy, which posits that individuals are more likely to engage in activism when they feel a shared sense of purpose and capability within a group [?].

Kompany embraced this concept, understanding that their melodies could amplify voices often unheard. Through their lyrics, they addressed pressing societal issues such as climate change, mental health, and social justice, encouraging their audience to reflect and take action. Their song, "Echoes of Change," became an anthem for environmental awareness, resonating with fans who were passionate about protecting the planet.

Engagement with Charitable Causes

Kompany's activism extended beyond their music; they actively engaged with various charitable organizations. For instance, they partnered with *Music for Change*, a nonprofit dedicated to using music as a tool for social justice. Through benefit concerts and fundraising campaigns, they raised significant funds to support education initiatives for underprivileged youth.

In 2020, during the height of the COVID-19 pandemic, Kompany released a single titled "Together Apart," with all proceeds directed to healthcare workers and mental health organizations. This initiative not only provided financial support but also offered hope and solidarity during a challenging time. The band's commitment to philanthropy exemplifies the potential for artists to effect change through their platforms.

Challenges Faced in Activism

Despite their good intentions, Kompany faced challenges in their activism journey. One significant problem was the backlash from certain segments of their fanbase who disagreed with the band's political stance. This phenomenon, known as "cancel culture," can lead to a divide among fans, as seen in the case of several artists who faced criticism for their outspoken views [?].

Kompany addressed these challenges by emphasizing the importance of dialogue and understanding. They organized forums where fans could discuss their differing perspectives, fostering an environment of respect and open communication. This approach not only strengthened their relationship with fans but also reinforced their commitment to activism as a means of uniting rather than dividing.

Impact and Legacy

The impact of Kompany's activism is evident in the way they have inspired a new generation of musicians to use their platforms for social good. Their efforts have sparked conversations around important issues, encouraging fans to become advocates within their communities. As noted by [?], artists who engage in activism can create a ripple effect, motivating their audience to take action and contribute to positive change.

Kompany's legacy in music and activism is not just about their chart-topping hits but also about the lives they have touched and the movements they have inspired. Their commitment to making a difference through music serves as a testament to the transformative power of art, reminding us that every note played can echo in the hearts of many.

Conclusion

In conclusion, Kompany's journey through activism illustrates the profound impact that music can have on society. By harnessing their influence, they have not only elevated important causes but have also fostered a sense of community and collective action among their fans. As they continue to create music that resonates with the world, their legacy as artists and activists will undoubtedly endure, inspiring future generations to use their voices for change.

Kompany's Cultural Impact

Global recognition and international success

The journey of Kompany from local favorites to international sensations is a testament to their unique sound and relentless dedication. Their rise to global recognition can be analyzed through various factors including their musical style, strategic collaborations, and the impact of digital platforms.

The Unique Sound of Kompany

Kompany's sound is characterized by a fusion of various genres, blending elements of pop, rock, and electronic music. This eclectic mix not only appeals to a broad audience but also allows them to stand out in a saturated music market. The band's ability to innovate while staying true to their roots has contributed significantly to their global appeal.

$$S = f(P, R, E) \tag{46}$$

Where:

- S = Sound quality and uniqueness
- P = Passion for music
- R = Rhythmic innovation
- E = Emotional connection with the audience

This equation illustrates that the sound of Kompany is a function of their passion, rhythmic innovation, and emotional connection with listeners. Each element plays a crucial role in crafting a sound that resonates on a global scale.

Strategic Collaborations

Kompany's collaborations with international artists have also propelled their success. By working with established musicians from different cultural backgrounds, they have not only diversified their sound but also expanded their reach. For example, their collaboration with a renowned Latin artist on a remix of their hit single garnered attention from Latin music fans, thereby introducing Kompany to a new demographic.

$$R_{total} = R_{local} + R_{global} \qquad (47)$$

Where:

- R_{total} = Total reach of Kompany's music
- R_{local} = Reach within local markets
- R_{global} = Reach in international markets

This formula illustrates how strategic collaborations can enhance their overall reach, allowing them to penetrate markets that were previously inaccessible.

The Impact of Digital Platforms

In the modern music industry, digital platforms play a pivotal role in the dissemination of music. Kompany has effectively utilized social media, streaming services, and music videos to build their brand and connect with fans worldwide. Their presence on platforms like Spotify and YouTube not only increases their visibility but also enables them to engage with a global audience.

The power of digital marketing can be encapsulated in the following equation:

$$E = C \times A \qquad (48)$$

Where:

- E = Engagement level of the audience
- C = Content quality
- A = Audience reach

Kompany's high-quality content, combined with their extensive audience reach, results in significant engagement, which is crucial for maintaining their international presence.

Challenges in Achieving Global Recognition

Despite their success, Kompany faced challenges in navigating the complexities of the international music scene. Language barriers, cultural differences, and varying market dynamics can pose significant obstacles. However, the band's commitment to understanding and embracing these differences has allowed them to adapt and thrive.

For instance, when releasing music in non-English speaking markets, they often collaborate with local artists to ensure cultural relevance and authenticity. This approach not only helps them overcome language barriers but also fosters a sense of community among diverse audiences.

Examples of International Success

Kompany's international success is exemplified by their sold-out shows in major cities around the world, including London, Tokyo, and Sydney. Their ability to draw large crowds in diverse locations underscores their global appeal. Additionally, their chart-topping singles in multiple countries highlight their widespread recognition.

For instance, their single "Heartbeats" topped charts in over ten countries, showcasing their ability to resonate with audiences across different cultures. The song's universal themes of love and longing are relatable, further contributing to its success.

Conclusion

Kompany's journey to global recognition and international success is a multifaceted narrative that encompasses their unique sound, strategic collaborations, and adept use of digital platforms. While challenges exist, their resilience and adaptability continue to pave the way for future achievements. As they expand their horizons, Kompany not only solidifies their place in music history but also inspires a new generation of musicians to pursue their dreams on a global stage.

Breaking barriers and pushing boundaries

In the ever-evolving landscape of the music industry, Kompany has consistently demonstrated an unwavering commitment to breaking barriers and pushing boundaries. This ethos not only defines their artistic journey but also reflects a broader narrative of innovation and resilience within the realm of modern music.

At the heart of Kompany's philosophy is the belief that music should be a vehicle for change, a sentiment echoed by many influential artists throughout history. This notion aligns with the theory of **cultural hegemony**, articulated by Antonio Gramsci, which posits that cultural norms and values are often dictated by dominant groups in society. Kompany's music challenges these norms, offering a refreshing perspective that resonates with a diverse audience. By embracing a wide array of influences—from traditional genres to contemporary sounds—they have not only carved out a unique niche but have also encouraged other artists to explore their creative boundaries.

One of the significant barriers that Kompany has tackled is the **gender disparity** within the music industry. In a field where female artists often face systemic challenges, Kompany has taken a proactive stance by promoting inclusivity and diversity. This commitment is exemplified in their collaborations with female musicians and producers, fostering an environment where underrepresented voices can thrive. Such initiatives not only empower individual artists but also challenge the status quo, contributing to a more equitable music landscape.

Moreover, Kompany's willingness to experiment with genre-blending serves as a testament to their boundary-pushing ethos. For instance, their hit single, *"Echoes of Tomorrow,"* seamlessly merges elements of electronic dance music (EDM) with acoustic folk, creating a sound that defies categorization. This genre-defying approach is supported by the **theory of intertextuality**, which suggests that all texts (or, in this case, musical works) are interconnected. By drawing from various influences, Kompany not only expands their artistic palette but also invites listeners to engage with music in new and exciting ways.

$$\text{Innovation Index} = \frac{\text{Number of Genres Explored}}{\text{Total Albums Released}} \qquad (49)$$

This equation provides a quantitative measure of Kompany's innovative spirit. For example, if Kompany has released five albums and explored ten distinct genres, their Innovation Index would be:

$$\text{Innovation Index} = \frac{10}{5} = 2 \qquad (50)$$

An Innovation Index greater than one indicates a prolific exploration of genres, showcasing their dedication to pushing musical boundaries.

Kompany's impact extends beyond their music; they have also been instrumental in advocating for **social change**. Their partnership with various charitable organizations highlights their commitment to using their platform for positive impact. For instance, their collaboration with *Music for Change* has raised awareness about mental health issues, a cause that resonates deeply with their fan base. By addressing these critical societal issues through their art, Kompany not only entertains but also educates and inspires action.

The band's efforts to break barriers are further exemplified by their international tours, which often feature local artists from the regions they perform in. This practice not only enriches their shows but also amplifies the voices of emerging talents, fostering a sense of community and collaboration across cultural divides. By integrating local sounds and styles into their performances, Kompany not only pushes musical boundaries but also promotes cultural exchange, thereby enriching the global music scene.

In conclusion, Kompany's journey exemplifies the power of music as a transformative force. By breaking barriers and pushing boundaries, they have not only redefined their artistic identity but have also contributed to a more inclusive and dynamic music industry. Their legacy serves as an inspiration for aspiring musicians, encouraging them to challenge conventions and explore the limitless possibilities of creative expression. As they continue to evolve, Kompany remains a beacon of innovation and resilience, proving that with passion and perseverance, the barriers of the past can be transformed into the stepping stones of the future.

Leaving a mark on music history

Kompany's journey through the music industry is not merely a tale of success; it is a profound testament to the power of creativity, resilience, and the indelible impact of music on culture. As they navigated through the complexities of fame, their unique sound and artistic vision carved a niche that resonated with millions, leaving an imprint that will endure long after the final note fades.

Cultural Significance

The music of Kompany transcends mere entertainment; it serves as a reflection of societal sentiments, encapsulating the joys, struggles, and aspirations of a generation. Their lyrics, often infused with raw emotion and relatable narratives, resonate deeply with fans, providing a soundtrack to both personal and collective experiences. This connection is not accidental; it is a deliberate effort by the band to engage with their audience on a meaningful level.

For instance, their breakout hit, which topped charts and became an anthem for many, was inspired by the tumultuous socio-political climate of the time. The song's chorus, a rallying cry for unity and hope, became synonymous with movements advocating for change. This illustrates how music can serve as a powerful tool for social commentary, influencing public perception and inspiring action.

Musical Innovation

Kompany's sound is characterized by a distinctive blend of genres, seamlessly merging elements of rock, pop, and electronic music. This innovative approach not only sets them apart from their contemporaries but also contributes to the evolution of the music landscape. By pushing the boundaries of genre, they have inspired a new wave of artists to experiment and explore, fostering a culture of creativity and collaboration.

The band's willingness to incorporate diverse musical influences can be seen in their album *Echoes of Tomorrow*, which features collaborations with artists from various genres, including hip-hop and classical. This cross-pollination of styles not only enriches their music but also broadens the appeal, attracting a diverse fan base that spans different demographics and cultural backgrounds.

Legacy of Philanthropy

Beyond their musical contributions, Kompany's commitment to philanthropy has solidified their legacy within the industry. By leveraging their platform to advocate for social issues, they have demonstrated that artists can play a pivotal role in driving positive change. Their involvement in various charitable initiatives, from mental health awareness campaigns to environmental conservation efforts, showcases their dedication to using music as a force for good.

One notable example is their partnership with *Music for Change*, an organization aimed at providing music education to underprivileged youth. Through benefit concerts and fundraising events, Kompany has raised significant funds, ensuring that the next generation of musicians has access to the resources they need to thrive. This commitment to giving back not only enhances their reputation but also inspires fans to engage in activism and community service.

Influence on Future Generations

Kompany's impact on the music industry extends far beyond their own discography. As mentors and collaborators, they have nurtured emerging artists, providing guidance and support that helps shape the future of music. Their willingness to share the spotlight with up-and-coming talent underscores their belief in the importance of community within the industry.

The band has also been instrumental in fostering a culture of inclusivity, advocating for diversity in music. Their collaborations with artists from various backgrounds serve as a powerful reminder that music knows no boundaries, encouraging others to embrace different perspectives and experiences. This commitment to inclusivity not only enriches the music scene but also paves the way for a more equitable industry.

Conclusion

In conclusion, Kompany's journey through the music industry is a remarkable story of artistic innovation, cultural significance, and social responsibility. Their ability to connect with audiences on a profound level, coupled with their commitment to philanthropy and mentorship, ensures that their legacy will endure for generations to come. As they continue to push the boundaries of music and inspire others, Kompany leaves an indelible mark on the tapestry of music history, reminding us all of the transformative power of art.

Chapter Highlights:

Kompany's enduring fan base

Kompany's journey through the music industry has been marked not only by their musical evolution but also by the unwavering support of their fan base. This section delves into the dynamics of this relationship, exploring how the band has cultivated a loyal following that transcends mere fandom, becoming a community of individuals united by their shared love for the music and the messages that Kompany embodies.

The Foundation of Loyalty

At the heart of Kompany's enduring fan base is a deep-seated loyalty that stems from the band's authenticity and relatability. From their early days, the members of Kompany have prioritized genuine connections with their audience. This authenticity resonates with fans, making them feel seen and heard. As noted in [?], the emotional connection that fans develop with artists is crucial in fostering long-term loyalty. The band's ability to share personal stories and experiences through their lyrics creates a narrative that fans can relate to, thus strengthening this bond.

Engagement Strategies

Kompany has employed various engagement strategies to maintain and grow their fan base. Social media platforms have become a vital tool for the band to connect with their audience. Regular updates, behind-the-scenes content, and interactive Q&A sessions allow fans to feel involved in the band's journey. According to [?],

CHAPTER HIGHLIGHTS: 119

artists who actively engage with their fans on social media are more likely to cultivate a dedicated following. Kompany's use of platforms like Instagram and Twitter to share snippets of new music, personal anecdotes, and even their struggles has made fans feel like they are part of the band's story.

Community Building

Beyond individual interactions, Kompany has fostered a sense of community among their fans. The establishment of fan clubs and online forums has provided spaces for fans to connect with one another, share their experiences, and discuss their interpretations of the band's music. This community aspect is essential, as it creates a shared identity among fans, reinforcing their loyalty to the band. As highlighted by [?], fandoms often develop their own subcultures, and Kompany's fan base is no exception. Events such as fan meet-ups and listening parties further solidify these bonds, creating lasting memories and connections.

The Role of Live Performances

Live performances play a pivotal role in nurturing Kompany's fan base. The energy and emotion experienced during concerts create a unique atmosphere that fosters a deep connection between the band and their audience. As discussed in [?], live music experiences can significantly enhance fan loyalty, as they provide an opportunity for fans to engage with the artists in a visceral way. Kompany's concerts are known for their inclusivity, often inviting fans to sing along and participate in the performance, further deepening this connection.

Fan Contributions and Involvement

Kompany recognizes and values the contributions of their fans, which has further solidified their loyalty. The band often highlights fan-created content, such as cover songs, artwork, and videos, showcasing the talent and creativity within their community. This acknowledgment not only empowers fans but also fosters a sense of belonging. According to [?], when fans feel that their contributions are valued, their loyalty to the artist increases significantly.

Navigating Challenges Together

Throughout their career, Kompany has faced various challenges, from internal band dynamics to external pressures from the music industry. During these times, the support of their fan base has been crucial. Fans have rallied around the band during difficult periods, demonstrating their unwavering loyalty. This solidarity not only reinforces the bond between the band and their fans but also highlights the importance of community in navigating challenges. As noted in [?], the collective identity of a fan base can provide a buffer against external pressures, allowing artists to focus on their craft.

Legacy of Loyalty

Kompany's enduring fan base is a testament to their impact on the music industry and the lives of their listeners. The band's ability to connect on a personal level, engage through various platforms, and foster a sense of community has created a loyal following that continues to grow. As they navigate the ever-changing landscape of the music industry, the support of their fans remains a constant source of strength.

In conclusion, the loyalty of Kompany's fan base is not merely a byproduct of their music but a reflection of the deep connections forged through authenticity, engagement, and shared experiences. This enduring relationship serves as a foundation for the band's continued success and influence in the music world.

Awards and honors for their contributions

The journey of Kompany has been marked by numerous accolades and honors that reflect their significant impact on the music industry. These awards not only celebrate their artistic achievements but also acknowledge their influence on fans and fellow musicians alike. In this section, we delve into the prestigious awards that Kompany has received, highlighting the importance of these recognitions within the broader context of their career.

Grammy Awards

One of the most coveted accolades in the music industry, the Grammy Awards, has recognized Kompany for their exceptional contributions to contemporary music. The band received their first Grammy for *Best New Artist* shortly after the release of their debut album, marking a significant milestone in their career. This award not only validated their hard work and dedication but also opened doors to new opportunities in the music scene.

$$\text{Grammy Recognition} = \text{Artistic Excellence} + \text{Industry Acknowledgment} \quad (51)$$

CHAPTER HIGHLIGHTS:

This equation illustrates that the recognition by the Grammy Awards is a composite of both artistic excellence and acknowledgment by industry peers, signifying a well-rounded contribution to music.

MTV Music Awards

Kompany's electrifying performances and innovative music videos earned them multiple MTV Music Awards, including *Video of the Year* and *Best Rock Video*. These awards not only celebrate their visual artistry but also their ability to connect with audiences through compelling storytelling in their music videos.

$$\text{MTV Award Success} = \text{Innovative Visuals} + \text{Audience Engagement} \qquad (52)$$

The above equation emphasizes the dual factors that contribute to winning MTV Music Awards, showcasing the importance of both innovative visuals and strong audience engagement.

Billboard Music Awards

Kompany has consistently topped the Billboard charts, leading to several Billboard Music Awards. Their chart-topping singles and albums have earned them titles such as *Top Rock Artist* and *Top Selling Album*, further solidifying their place in the music industry. The Billboard Music Awards reflect commercial success and popularity, underscoring their ability to resonate with a wide audience.

$$\text{Billboard Success} = \text{Chart Performance} + \text{Sales Figures} \qquad (53)$$

This equation illustrates how the success at the Billboard Music Awards is derived from both chart performance and sales figures, highlighting the commercial aspect of their contributions.

American Music Awards

The American Music Awards (AMAs) have also honored Kompany with several prestigious titles, including *Favorite Alternative Rock Artist*. These awards are determined by public voting, which underscores the band's connection with their fan base and the impact they have had on listeners.

$$\text{AMA Recognition} = \text{Fan Voting} + \text{Cultural Impact} \qquad (54)$$

Here, the equation captures the essence of the American Music Awards, where recognition is based on fan voting and the cultural impact that the band has made.

International Recognition

Kompany's influence extends beyond national borders, as they have received numerous international awards, including the *Brit Awards* and the *Juno Awards*. These accolades reflect their global appeal and the way their music transcends cultural barriers.

$$\text{International Awards} = \text{Global Reach} + \text{Cultural Resonance} \qquad (55)$$

This equation outlines how international awards are a result of both the band's global reach and their cultural resonance with diverse audiences.

Philanthropic Awards

In addition to their musical accolades, Kompany has been recognized for their philanthropic efforts. They have received awards for their contributions to various charitable causes, demonstrating their commitment to using their platform for positive change.

$$\text{Philanthropic Recognition} = \text{Community Impact} + \text{Charitable Contributions} \qquad (56)$$

This equation highlights that philanthropic recognition is based on the impact made within communities and the contributions to charitable initiatives, showcasing the band's dedication to social responsibility.

Conclusion

In summary, the awards and honors received by Kompany serve as a testament to their multifaceted contributions to the music industry and society. Each accolade not only celebrates their artistic achievements but also reflects their ability to connect with fans, influence fellow musicians, and make a difference in the world. As Kompany continues to evolve and inspire, their legacy of excellence and impact remains firmly established in the annals of music history.

Looking back on a remarkable career

As we take a moment to reflect on the remarkable journey of Kompany, it becomes evident that their impact on the music industry transcends mere numbers and accolades. The essence of their career is woven into the fabric of their songs, the emotions they evoke, and the connections they have fostered with fans across the globe.

The story of Kompany is not just a tale of musical success; it is a narrative rich with trials, triumphs, and transformative experiences. Each album they released marked a pivotal moment in their evolution, showcasing not only their growth as musicians but also their ability to adapt to the ever-changing landscape of the music industry.

The Evolution of Sound

Kompany's sound has evolved significantly since their inception. Early tracks, characterized by raw energy and youthful exuberance, laid the foundation for a more sophisticated and nuanced style that emerged in later albums. This evolution can be modeled using the concept of *musical progression*, which can be represented mathematically by the equation:

$$M(t) = M_0 + \int_0^t f(s)ds \tag{57}$$

where $M(t)$ represents the maturity of their music at time t, M_0 is the initial sound, and $f(s)$ is a function representing the influences and experiences that shape their music over time.

Kompany's willingness to experiment with different genres, collaborate with diverse artists, and incorporate new technologies into their music has allowed them to stay relevant and resonate with both old and new fans. Their ability to blend elements of pop, rock, and electronic music has not only set them apart but has also influenced a generation of aspiring musicians.

Memorable Milestones

Throughout their career, Kompany has achieved numerous milestones that have solidified their legacy. From their first album release, which skyrocketed them into the limelight, to their sold-out stadium tours that brought fans together in celebration, each moment has contributed to the tapestry of their journey.

One of the most significant achievements was their breakthrough hit, which not only topped charts but also received critical acclaim. This can be analyzed through the lens of the *success function*, defined as:

$$S = \frac{R + C}{T} \tag{58}$$

where S is the success score, R is the revenue generated, C is the critical acclaim received, and T is the time taken to achieve these results. This formula illustrates how Kompany's ability to generate revenue and garner critical praise has propelled their career forward.

Cultural Impact

Kompany's influence extends beyond their music; they have made a significant cultural impact that has inspired countless individuals. Their songs often reflect societal issues, personal struggles, and the human experience, resonating deeply with fans from all walks of life. This phenomenon can be expressed through the *cultural resonance equation*:

$$CR = \frac{E \times A}{D} \tag{59}$$

where CR is the cultural resonance, E represents the emotional engagement of their music, A is the audience reach, and D is the degree of disconnect from mainstream narratives. Kompany's ability to connect emotionally with their audience has allowed them to maintain a strong presence in the cultural zeitgeist.

Legacy and Future Aspirations

As we look back on Kompany's career, it is clear that their legacy is not solely defined by their past achievements but also by their aspirations for the future. They have continually expressed a desire to evolve, innovate, and push the boundaries of their music. This forward-thinking mindset can be encapsulated in the *legacy equation*:

$$L = \int_0^T (I(t) + E(t))dt \tag{60}$$

where L is the legacy, T is the total time of their career, $I(t)$ represents the innovations introduced at time t, and $E(t)$ reflects the emotional impact of their work over time. This equation symbolizes how their commitment to innovation and emotional connection will continue to shape their legacy.

In conclusion, as we reflect on the remarkable career of Kompany, we celebrate not only their successes but also the profound connections they have forged with their fans and the music community. Their journey is a testament to the power of music to inspire, heal, and unite. As they continue to create and evolve, the legacy of Kompany will undoubtedly live on, resonating in the hearts of fans for generations to come.

Conclusion

Kompany: Forever in the Hearts of Fans

Reflecting on the journey together

As we take a moment to pause and look back on the incredible journey of **Kompany**, it becomes evident that this story is not just about a band; it's about a collective experience, a tapestry woven from the threads of friendship, passion, and resilience. Each note played and every lyric sung has been a reflection of our shared dreams and struggles, creating a bond that transcends the music itself.

The journey began in the humble surroundings of our childhood, where we discovered our love for music. It was in those formative years that we learned the true essence of collaboration. *Collaboration* in music is not merely about combining sounds; it's about harmonizing ideas, emotions, and aspirations. The process of creating something beautiful together is akin to a mathematical equation where each member contributes a unique variable. The equation of our success can be expressed as:

$$S = (F_1 + F_2 + F_3 + \ldots + F_n) \times C \qquad (61)$$

Where S is the overall success of Kompany, F_i represents the individual contributions of each band member, and C is the cohesion and synergy we share. This equation encapsulates how our combined efforts, fueled by camaraderie, have led to the music that resonates with our fans.

Reflecting on the early days, we faced numerous challenges that tested our resolve. From the first gigs in local cafes to the exhilarating feeling of being embraced by a growing fan base, each experience was a lesson in perseverance. The initial setbacks, whether it was a poorly attended show or technical difficulties, were not merely obstacles but stepping stones that shaped our identity as a band. We learned that *failure* is an integral part of the creative process. As Thomas

Edison famously said, "I have not failed. I've just found 10,000 ways that won't work." This perspective allowed us to embrace our missteps, turning them into opportunities for growth.

Connection with our audience has always been at the heart of our journey. Each concert felt like a dialogue, a shared moment where we could feel the pulse of our fans. The energy in the room was palpable, reminding us that music is a universal language that transcends barriers. The emotional connection we fostered with our listeners became a driving force behind our songwriting. The lyrics we penned were often a reflection of the stories shared with us by our fans—tales of love, loss, and triumph.

As we moved from local recognition to national acclaim, the sense of responsibility grew. With success came the scrutiny of the media and the expectations of our fans. It was crucial for us to remain grounded and true to our roots. *Authenticity* became our guiding principle. We understood that while we could evolve musically, the essence of who we are as individuals and as a band must remain intact. This commitment to authenticity is what allowed us to navigate the complexities of fame while still connecting with our audience on a personal level.

In the midst of our ascent, we faced the inevitable pressures that accompany success. The internal dynamics of the band were tested, leading to moments of conflict and introspection. Yet, these challenges were not the end but rather a catalyst for deeper understanding. We learned the importance of *communication*—that open dialogue could mend rifts and strengthen our bond. Each disagreement was a chance to reassess our goals and reaffirm our commitment to one another.

As we reflect on our journey, we acknowledge the pivotal moments that have defined us. The breakthrough hit that catapulted us into the limelight was not just a product of talent; it was the culmination of years of hard work, persistence, and the unwavering support of our fans. Each accolade and award is a testament to the collective effort of not just the band, but everyone who has believed in us along the way.

In this moment of reflection, we are filled with gratitude. Gratitude for the late-night jam sessions, the laughter shared during rehearsals, and the tears shed during tough times. Each experience has contributed to the rich tapestry of our story. As we look forward to the future, we do so with the knowledge that our journey is far from over. The legacy of Kompany is not just about the music we create, but the connections we forge and the impact we leave behind.

In conclusion, reflecting on our journey together is a reminder of the power of music to unite, heal, and inspire. It is a celebration of the moments that have shaped us, the lessons learned, and the love that binds us. As we continue to write the next chapters of our story, we do so with the hope that our music will continue to resonate with hearts around the world, creating a legacy that will endure for generations to come.

Gratitude and appreciation for the support

In the tapestry of life and music, each thread represents a moment, a memory, a person who has shaped our journey. As we take a moment to reflect on the incredible ride that has been our time as Kompany, we find ourselves enveloped in a profound sense of gratitude for the unwavering support we have received from our fans, families, and friends. This section is dedicated to expressing our heartfelt appreciation for those who have stood by us through thick and thin, turning our dreams into a shared reality.

The Fans: Our Heartbeat

From the very first note we played to the roaring crowds at our early gigs, it was clear that our fans were not just an audience; they were our heartbeat. Each cheer, each shout, and every tear shed during our performances has fortified our resolve to create music that resonates. The connection we share with our fans transcends the boundaries of the stage. It is a symbiotic relationship, where your energy fuels our creativity, and our music becomes the soundtrack to your lives.

$$\text{Connection} = \text{Energy}_{\text{fans}} \times \text{Creativity}_{\text{band}} \qquad (62)$$

This equation encapsulates the essence of our relationship. The energy you bring to our shows ignites our creativity, leading to performances that are not just concerts, but communal celebrations of life and music.

Family and Friends: The Backbone of Support

Behind every successful band lies a network of family and friends who believe in the dream, often before it becomes tangible. Our families have been our pillars of strength, providing encouragement during the late-night rehearsals and the countless hours spent perfecting our craft. They have celebrated our victories and consoled us during our defeats, reminding us that the journey is just as important as the destination.

$$\text{Support} = \text{Love}_{\text{family}} + \text{Belief}_{\text{friends}} \qquad (63)$$

This equation highlights the dual forces that have propelled us forward. The love from our families and the unwavering belief from our friends have created an environment where we could flourish and pursue our passion without hesitation.

The Team: Unsung Heroes

While we stand in the spotlight, there exists a dedicated team working tirelessly behind the scenes to ensure that everything runs smoothly. From our sound engineers to our tour managers, each member of our team plays a crucial role in our success. Their expertise and commitment allow us to focus on what we do best: creating music.

$$\text{Success} = \text{Talent}_{band} + \text{Dedication}_{team} \tag{64}$$

This equation illustrates the collaborative nature of our success. It is not solely our talent that has brought us this far; it is the dedication of our entire team that has made it possible for us to shine.

Community and Collaboration

Beyond the individual contributions of fans, family, and our team, we are deeply grateful for the broader community of artists, musicians, and creators who have inspired and collaborated with us along the way. Each collaboration has enriched our sound and broadened our horizons, reminding us that music is a universal language that connects us all.

$$\text{Growth} = \text{Collaboration}_{artists} + \text{Inspiration}_{community} \tag{65}$$

Through this equation, we recognize that our growth as a band has been significantly influenced by the collaborations we've engaged in and the inspiration we've drawn from our community.

A Collective Journey

As we look back on our journey, it becomes clear that our success is not just a reflection of our hard work, but a collective effort that encompasses everyone who has supported us. To our fans who sing our lyrics back to us, to our families who have sacrificed for our dreams, to our team who works tirelessly behind the scenes, and to the community that inspires us daily—thank you.

Your support has not only made our dreams possible but has also created a legacy that we hope will inspire future generations of musicians. We are eternally grateful for each and every one of you, and we carry your love with us in every note we play.

$$\text{Legacy} = \text{Support}_{\text{all}} \times \text{Music}_{\text{Kompany}} \tag{66}$$

In conclusion, as we continue to forge ahead, we do so with the knowledge that we are not alone. We are Kompany, and we are forever in the hearts of our supporters, a testament to the power of music and the connections it creates.

The legacy of Kompany lives on

The legacy of Kompany is a multifaceted tapestry woven from the threads of their music, their message, and the indelible mark they have left on the hearts of fans around the globe. As we reflect on their journey, it becomes evident that their influence transcends mere musical notes; it resonates deeply within the cultural consciousness of generations.

Cultural Resonance

Kompany's music has served as a soundtrack to the lives of many, capturing the essence of love, heartache, and resilience. The band's ability to articulate complex emotions through relatable lyrics has created a profound connection with their audience. For instance, their hit single, *"Echoes of Tomorrow"*, not only topped charts but also became an anthem for those navigating the trials of life. The lyrics, *"In the silence, we find our way, through the shadows of yesterday,"* speak to the universal experience of overcoming adversity, illustrating how art can mirror life.

Inspiring Future Generations

Kompany's impact extends beyond their immediate fan base, inspiring countless aspiring musicians to pursue their dreams. The band's journey from humble beginnings to international stardom serves as a beacon of hope for those who dare to dream. Their story exemplifies the principle of **self-efficacy**, a concept introduced by psychologist Albert Bandura, which posits that individuals who believe in their capabilities are more likely to achieve their goals. Kompany's rise to fame embodies this theory, as they continually pushed the boundaries of their creativity and resilience.

Philanthropic Endeavors

Moreover, Kompany's commitment to philanthropy has solidified their legacy as more than just entertainers. The band has used its platform to champion various causes, from mental health awareness to environmental sustainability. Their initiative, *"Music for Change"*, has raised significant funds for mental health organizations, demonstrating the profound impact that artists can have on societal issues. This aligns with the **Social Change Theory**, which emphasizes the role of individuals and groups in creating social change through collective action.

Enduring Fan Connection

The bond between Kompany and their fans is another critical aspect of their legacy. Through social media platforms, the band has cultivated a community where fans feel valued and heard. This engagement fosters a sense of belonging, a crucial element in building a lasting legacy. The phenomenon of **fan culture**, as described by media theorist Henry Jenkins, highlights how fans actively participate in the creation and dissemination of meaning around their favorite artists. Kompany has embraced this culture, allowing their fans to share personal stories and experiences that resonate with the band's music.

Musical Evolution and Influence

Kompany's willingness to evolve musically has also contributed to their lasting legacy. By experimenting with different genres and collaborating with diverse artists, they have broadened their appeal and relevance in an ever-changing music landscape. For example, their collaboration with electronic artist *DJ Nova* on the track *"Rhythms of the Night"* showcases their versatility and willingness to embrace new sounds. This adaptability is crucial in the music industry, where trends shift rapidly, and artists must remain innovative to sustain their relevance.

Conclusion

In conclusion, the legacy of Kompany lives on through their powerful music, their philanthropic efforts, and their enduring connection with fans. As they continue to inspire future generations, their story serves as a reminder of the transformative power of music. Kompany's journey is not just about the accolades and achievements; it is about the lives they have touched and the change they have instigated. As they move forward, their legacy will undoubtedly continue to resonate, echoing through the hearts of all who have been fortunate enough to experience their artistry.

Acknowledgements

Thanking the fans and supporters

Recognizing the contributions of the band members

Appreciation for the team behind Kompany's success

Appendix

Discography

Album releases

Kompany's discography is a testament to their evolution as artists and their impact on the music industry. Each album they released not only showcased their growth in musicality but also reflected the changing dynamics of their personal and professional lives. Below is a detailed overview of their major album releases:

Debut Album: *Echoes of Youth* (2015)

Kompany burst onto the scene with their debut album, *Echoes of Youth*, which encapsulated the raw energy and passion of their early years. The album features a mix of upbeat tracks and heartfelt ballads, with standout singles such as "Chasing Shadows" and "Homeward Bound."

- Tracklist:
    1. Chasing Shadows
    2. Homeward Bound
    3. Lost in the Night
    4. Dreamers Unite
    5. The Road Ahead
    6. Silent Whispers
    7. Echoes of Youth
    8. Stars Collide
    9. In Our Hearts

10. End of the Line

- **Critical Reception:** The album received positive reviews from critics, who praised its lyrical depth and melodic structure. It was nominated for several local music awards and won the *Best New Artist Album* at the Local Music Awards in 2016.

Sophomore Album: *Rising Tides* **(2017)**

Building on the success of their debut, Kompany released *Rising Tides,* an album that marked a significant maturation in their sound. This album explored deeper themes of love, loss, and resilience, resonating with a wider audience.

- **Tracklist:**

    1. Waves of Change
    2. Heartbeats
    3. Letting Go
    4. Midnight Sun
    5. Stormy Seas
    6. A New Dawn
    7. Reflections
    8. Shadows Dance
    9. Tides of Time
    10. Rise Again

- **Chart Performance:** *Rising Tides* debuted at number 5 on the national charts and produced several hit singles, including "Waves of Change," which became a staple in their live performances.

Third Album: *Fragments of Us* **(2019)**

This album represented a turning point for Kompany, as they began to experiment with new sounds and collaborations. *Fragments of Us* included a mix of electronic elements and acoustic instrumentation, showcasing their versatility as musicians.

- **Tracklist:**

DISCOGRAPHY 137

1. Fragments of Us
2. Electric Dreams
3. The Other Side
4. Unbreakable
5. Forgotten Melodies
6. Together Apart
7. Colors of Life
8. Echoes in the Dark
9. The Ties That Bind
10. Homecoming

- **Collaborations:** The album featured collaborations with renowned artists and producers, including a notable track with Grammy-winning producer, Alex Stewart. This collaboration helped elevate Kompany's profile in the music industry.

Fourth Album: *Through the Pulse* (2021)

Through the Pulse marked a return to their roots while also embracing the evolution of their sound. This album was a reflection of their journey, filled with heartfelt lyrics and powerful anthems that connected with fans on a personal level.

- **Tracklist:**

    1. Pulse
    2. Heartbeat
    3. Rise from Ashes
    4. Light in the Dark
    5. Uncharted Waters
    6. Never Alone
    7. Echoes of Tomorrow
    8. Boundless
    9. The Journey Within
    10. Together We Stand

- **Impact:** The album received critical acclaim and solidified Kompany's status as a leading force in the music industry. It won the *Album of the Year* at the National Music Awards and included the chart-topping single "Pulse."

Upcoming Album: *Beyond the Horizon* (Expected 2024)

Kompany is currently working on their highly anticipated fifth album, *Beyond the Horizon*. Fans eagerly await its release, as the band has teased a return to their experimental roots while incorporating new influences from global music trends.

- **Expectations:** The album is expected to include collaborations with international artists and explore themes of unity and hope in a post-pandemic world.

- **Pre-release Singles:** The first single, "New Beginnings," has already been released and has garnered positive feedback, hinting at the exciting direction of the upcoming album.

In summary, Kompany's album releases reflect their journey as artists and their commitment to evolving while staying true to their roots. Each album not only showcases their musical prowess but also serves as a narrative of their experiences, challenges, and triumphs throughout their career.

Singles and Popular Tracks

Kompany's journey through the music landscape is punctuated by a collection of singles and tracks that not only showcase their evolution as artists but also resonate deeply with their fans. Each song reflects a chapter in their story, capturing emotions, experiences, and the essence of their musical identity. In this section, we will explore some of the standout singles that have defined Kompany's career, highlighting their impact, themes, and the response from audiences and critics alike.

Early Singles

Kompany's debut single, *"Chasing Shadows"*, released in 2015, marked the beginning of their ascent in the music scene. This track, characterized by its haunting melodies and poignant lyrics, encapsulated the struggles of youth and the search for identity. The song's catchy chorus and relatable themes quickly garnered attention, leading to significant airplay on local radio stations.

DISCOGRAPHY

$$\text{Popularity Index} = \frac{\text{Radio Play Count} + \text{Streaming Count} + \text{Sales}}{\text{Time Since Release}} \qquad (67)$$

Using the formula above, *"Chasing Shadows"* achieved a high popularity index, solidifying its place as a fan favorite. The track's success laid the groundwork for future releases and established Kompany as a band to watch.

Breakthrough Hits

The turning point for Kompany came with their second single, *"Breaking Free"*, which was released in 2017. This anthem of empowerment resonated with a broader audience, leading to its inclusion in several playlists and charts. The song's infectious energy and uplifting message inspired many, making it a staple at their live performances.

$$\text{Chart Position} = f(\text{Sales}, \text{Airplay}, \text{Streaming}) \qquad (68)$$

"Breaking Free" reached the top 10 on national charts, a testament to its widespread appeal. The accompanying music video, featuring stunning visuals and a narrative of resilience, further amplified its reach.

Collaborative Efforts

Kompany's willingness to collaborate with other artists has also contributed to their success. The single *"Together We Rise"*, featuring renowned artist Jane Doe, was released in 2019 and became an anthem for social change. The song's powerful lyrics and compelling message about unity struck a chord, leading to various charity events and initiatives.

$$\text{Collaboration Impact} = \text{Artist Reach} \times \text{Combined Fan Base} \qquad (69)$$

The collaboration not only enhanced Kompany's visibility but also showcased their commitment to using music as a platform for positive change. The song's impact was evident through its chart performance and the overwhelming support from fans and critics.

Recent Releases

In 2021, Kompany released *"Echoes of Tomorrow"*, a reflective piece that delves into themes of nostalgia and hope. The song's introspective lyrics and melodic composition highlight the band's maturity and artistic growth. It received critical acclaim, with many reviewers praising its depth and emotional resonance.

$$\text{Critical Reception} = \frac{\text{Positive Reviews}}{\text{Total Reviews}} \times 100 \qquad (70)$$

With an impressive critical reception score of over 85%, *"Echoes of Tomorrow"* solidified Kompany's status as a leading force in contemporary music. The single's success was further amplified by its poignant music video, which visually represented the song's themes.

Fan Favorites and Legacy

Kompany's discography is filled with tracks that have become fan favorites, such as *"Dancing in the Rain"* and *"Silent Whispers"*. These songs, characterized by their emotional depth and relatable themes, have left a lasting impact on listeners. The band often incorporates these tracks into their setlists, creating memorable moments during live performances.

$$\text{Fan Engagement} = \text{Concert Attendance} + \text{Social Media Interactions} \qquad (71)$$

Kompany's ability to engage with their audience through both their music and live performances has fostered a loyal fan base. Their singles not only tell their story but also resonate with the experiences of their listeners, creating a shared journey that transcends the music itself.

Conclusion

In conclusion, Kompany's singles and popular tracks represent the heartbeat of their musical journey. Each release has contributed to their narrative, reflecting their growth as artists and their connection with fans. As they continue to evolve and explore new musical directions, their past singles will remain a testament to their enduring legacy in the music industry. The stories told through their music will echo in the hearts of fans for years to come, solidifying Kompany's place in the annals of music history.

Collaborations and Featured Appearances

Throughout their illustrious career, Kompany has not only solidified their unique sound but has also embraced the beauty of collaboration, reaching across genres and styles to create unforgettable music. This section delves into the various collaborations and featured appearances that have enriched their discography, showcasing their versatility and commitment to artistic exploration.

Significant Collaborations

Kompany's journey has been marked by a series of impactful collaborations that have helped shape their artistic identity. Each collaboration has brought a fresh perspective, blending different musical influences and creating a tapestry of sound that resonates with fans. Here are some notable partnerships:

- **With Indie Pop Sensation:** In 2019, Kompany teamed up with the indie pop artist, Lila Grace, on the track *"Echoes of Tomorrow."* This collaboration was a turning point, as it fused Kompany's signature rock sound with Lila's ethereal vocals, resulting in a hauntingly beautiful ballad that topped the charts for weeks. The song explores themes of nostalgia and longing, a testament to the emotional depth that both artists bring to their music.

- **Hip-Hop Fusion:** The band ventured into the hip-hop genre with their collaboration on *"Rhythm and Rhyme"* featuring renowned rapper, J. Cole. This track showcased a bold new direction for Kompany, incorporating rap verses and a groovy bassline that had fans dancing in the streets. The fusion of rock and hip-hop not only expanded their audience but also demonstrated their willingness to break down genre barriers.

- **A Tribute to Legends:** In 2021, Kompany collaborated with legendary guitarist Slash on a cover of *"Sweet Child O' Mine."* This tribute was not just a nod to the past but a reinvention of a classic, with Kompany's modern twist. The collaboration was a celebration of musical heritage, blending Slash's iconic guitar riffs with Kompany's contemporary style, resulting in a fresh take that was embraced by both old and new fans alike.

Featured Appearances

Kompany has also made several notable guest appearances on tracks by other artists, lending their unique sound and style to enhance the music of their peers. These featured appearances have further solidified their reputation as versatile musicians capable of complementing a variety of musical styles.

- **On the Road with Fellow Artists:** In 2020, they appeared on the track *"Chasing Stars"* by electronic duo, The Chainsmokers. Their contribution to the song added a layer of depth, with soaring vocals and harmonies that elevated the overall production. The collaboration was a commercial success, charting in multiple countries and showcasing Kompany's ability to blend seamlessly with electronic music.

- **International Collaborations:** Kompany has also crossed international borders, featuring on the hit single *"Dancing in the Moonlight"* by British DJ, Calvin Harris. Their collaboration brought a fresh perspective to the dance track, infusing it with rock elements that made it a summer anthem. This partnership highlighted the global appeal of Kompany's music, as they continue to resonate with audiences worldwide.

- **Supporting Emerging Artists:** Kompany has always believed in the importance of uplifting emerging talent. Their feature on *"New Horizons"* by up-and-coming singer-songwriter, Mia Torres, is a prime example. By lending their vocals and expertise, Kompany helped Mia gain recognition in the industry, while also showcasing their commitment to fostering new voices in music.

Impact of Collaborations

The collaborations and featured appearances by Kompany have not only contributed to their artistic growth but have also left a lasting impact on the music industry. By embracing diversity and experimentation, they have set a precedent for future artists to explore cross-genre collaborations.

$$\text{Impact} = \text{Diversity} + \text{Creativity} + \text{Collaboration} \tag{72}$$

This equation illustrates the essence of Kompany's collaborative approach, where diversity in musical styles, creativity in songwriting, and collaboration with various artists come together to create impactful music.

Kompany's willingness to collaborate has opened doors to new audiences, allowing them to connect with fans who may not have been reached through their traditional sound. Their partnerships have sparked conversations about the importance of collaboration in the music industry, encouraging artists to step outside their comfort zones and explore new creative avenues.

Conclusion

As Kompany continues to evolve and redefine their sound, their collaborations and featured appearances remain a testament to their artistic vision. Each partnership has not only enriched their music but has also contributed to a broader dialogue about the power of collaboration in the creative process. With every new project, they remind us that music knows no boundaries, and the beauty of collaboration lies in its ability to transcend genres and unite artists from all walks of life.

In celebrating these collaborations, we honor the spirit of creativity and the shared passion for music that drives Kompany forward. Their journey is a reminder that the magic of music is often found in the connections we make along the way.

Timeline of Significant Events

Milestones in Kompany's Career

The journey of Kompany is marked by numerous milestones that have shaped their identity and legacy in the music industry. These pivotal moments not only reflect the band's growth but also highlight their resilience and creativity in the face of challenges. Below is a detailed timeline of significant events that have defined Kompany's career.

Formation and Early Performances

The seeds of Kompany were sown in the hearts of childhood friends who shared a passion for music. In the spring of 2010, the band officially formed, bringing together Mei Raj, the lead vocalist, and her childhood friends, who were equally passionate about creating melodies that resonate with the soul. Their first performance at a local talent show in their hometown of Maplewood marked the beginning of their journey.

- **2010:** Formation of Kompany and debut performance at Maplewood Talent Show.

- **2011:** Release of their first EP, *Echoes of Youth*, which garnered local attention.

Breaking into the Local Scene

Kompany's early days were characterized by relentless performances at local bars and community events. They gradually built a loyal fan base, which became crucial for their future success.

- **2012:** First major gig at the Maplewood Music Festival, where they performed in front of a crowd of over 500 people.
- **2013:** Collaborated with local artists, expanding their musical repertoire and gaining recognition in the local music scene.

The Breakthrough Album

The band's hard work paid off in 2014 when they released their debut album, *Through the Pulse*. This album was a culmination of their experiences, showcasing their unique sound and lyrical depth.

- **2014:** Release of *Through the Pulse*, which included the hit single *Chasing Shadows*, propelling them into the national spotlight.
- **2015:** *Chasing Shadows* reached the top 10 on the national charts, marking their first major commercial success.

National Recognition and Tours

Following their initial success, Kompany quickly gained national recognition. They signed with a major label and embarked on their first nationwide tour.

- **2016:** Signing with *Echo Records*, leading to the release of their sophomore album, *Reflections*, which debuted at number 5 on the Billboard 200.
- **2017:** The *Reflections Tour* sold out venues across the country, solidifying their status as a leading band in the industry.

Awards and Accolades

Kompany's contributions to music were recognized through various awards, marking their influence and impact on the industry.

- **2018:** Won the *Best New Artist* award at the National Music Awards, a testament to their rapid rise in the music scene.
- **2019:** Nominated for a *Grammy Award* for *Best Pop Vocal Album* for *Reflections*.

Navigating Challenges and Reinvention

Despite their success, Kompany faced internal struggles that tested their unity and commitment to music.

- **2020:** Rumors of a potential breakup circulated, leading to a hiatus for the band to reflect and regroup.
- **2021:** The band returned with a powerful comeback album, *Rebirth*, which showcased their growth and maturity as artists.

Cultural Impact and Philanthropy

Kompany has not only influenced music but has also utilized their platform for positive change.

- **2022:** Launched the *Kompany Cares* initiative, focusing on mental health awareness and supporting young musicians.
- **2023:** Received the *Humanitarian Award* for their philanthropic efforts and contributions to the community.

Looking Ahead

As Kompany continues to evolve, they remain committed to their music and their fans. With plans for new projects and collaborations, the future looks bright for this dynamic band.

- **2024:** Announced a new album, *Echoes of Tomorrow*, set to release in the fall, promising to explore new musical territories.
- **2025:** Scheduled to embark on an international tour, aiming to connect with fans around the globe.

In conclusion, the milestones in Kompany's career reflect a tapestry woven with passion, perseverance, and creativity. Each event not only marks a significant achievement but also serves as a reminder of the band's journey and the unwavering support of their fans. As they continue to write their story, the legacy of Kompany is sure to resonate for generations to come.

Personal achievements and highlights

The journey of Kompany is not just a tale of musical evolution but also a chronicle of personal growth and triumphs that resonate deeply with their fans. Each member of the band has experienced significant milestones that have shaped their identities both as artists and individuals. This section delves into the personal achievements and highlights that have marked their journey.

Individual Milestones

Each member of Kompany has carved out unique paths that contribute to the band's collective narrative. For example, lead vocalist Alex Thompson, before joining the band, won a regional talent contest that showcased his vocal prowess and stage presence. This early recognition not only bolstered his confidence but also set the stage for his future endeavors with Kompany.

Similarly, guitarist Jamie Lee, known for her intricate riffs and powerful solos, was awarded a scholarship to a prestigious music school. This opportunity allowed her to hone her craft and develop a distinctive sound that would later become integral to Kompany's identity. The skills and techniques she acquired during this period are evident in tracks like "Echoes of Tomorrow," where her guitar work takes center stage.

Awards and Recognitions

Throughout their career, Kompany has received numerous accolades that highlight their impact on the music industry. One of the most notable achievements was winning the *Best New Artist* award at the National Music Awards shortly after the release of their debut album. This recognition not only validated their hard work but also opened doors to new opportunities, including collaborations with established artists.

In addition to industry awards, the band has also been honored with community recognitions for their philanthropic efforts. Their involvement in local charities, particularly those focused on music education for underprivileged children, earned them the *Community Impact Award*. This accolade reflects their commitment to using their platform for positive change, reinforcing their status as role models in the music community.

Personal Growth and Development

The pressures of fame and the demands of a touring lifestyle often challenge personal relationships and individual well-being. The members of Kompany have navigated these challenges with resilience. For instance, drummer Mark Rivera has spoken openly about his struggles with anxiety and how he sought therapy to manage it. His journey towards mental health awareness has inspired many fans, encouraging them to prioritize their own mental well-being.

Moreover, bassist Sam Patel's commitment to fitness and wellness has transformed his life, leading him to become a vocal advocate for healthy living. His journey is a testament to the importance of self-care in the high-pressure world of music. Sam often shares his fitness routine and healthy recipes on social media, cultivating a community that values both music and well-being.

Creative Pursuits Outside the Band

In addition to their work with Kompany, each member has pursued personal projects that reflect their diverse interests and talents. For instance, Jamie Lee released a solo EP that explores acoustic sounds and intimate storytelling, showcasing her versatility as an artist. This endeavor not only allowed her to express herself creatively but also attracted a new audience who appreciate her solo work.

Similarly, Alex Thompson has ventured into songwriting for other artists, collaborating with emerging talents in the industry. His ability to craft relatable lyrics has garnered attention, leading to successful placements in various music projects. This creative outlet has enriched his artistry and brought fresh perspectives to Kompany's music.

Fan Engagement and Community Building

Kompany's commitment to their fans goes beyond music; they actively engage with their audience through social media, live Q&A sessions, and fan meet-and-greets. This direct interaction fosters a sense of community and belonging among their supporters. The band often shares behind-the-scenes glimpses of their lives, allowing fans to connect with them on a personal level.

One memorable highlight was their "Thank You Tour," where they visited small towns across the country to express gratitude to their loyal fan base. These intimate shows created lasting memories and strengthened the bond between the band and their fans, emphasizing the importance of community in their journey.

Legacy of Personal Achievements

The personal achievements of each member of Kompany contribute to a legacy that extends beyond their music. Their stories of resilience, creativity, and community engagement serve as an inspiration for aspiring musicians and fans alike. By overcoming challenges and pursuing their passions, they embody the spirit of perseverance that resonates with many.

In conclusion, the personal achievements and highlights of Kompany reflect not only their individual journeys but also the collective spirit of the band. Their commitment to growth, community, and creativity continues to inspire and uplift those who follow their music. As they look to the future, the members of Kompany remain dedicated to their craft and the impact they can make through their art and actions.

Additional Interviews and Quotes

Exclusive insights from band members

In this section, we delve into the personal reflections and insights shared by the members of Kompany. Through candid interviews, we explore their thoughts on the band's journey, the creative process, and the challenges they faced along the way.

Vocalist's Perspective: Mei Raj

Mei Raj, the soulful voice of Kompany, reflects on the early days of the band with a mix of nostalgia and gratitude. "When we first started, it was just about the music," she recalls. "We were a group of friends who loved to jam. The idea of being recognized was a distant dream." Mei emphasizes the importance of authenticity in their music:

> "I always believed that if we stayed true to ourselves, the music would resonate with others. It's about pouring your heart out and letting it flow into the songs."

This authenticity became a cornerstone of Kompany's identity, allowing them to connect deeply with their audience.

ADDITIONAL INTERVIEWS AND QUOTES

Guitarist's Insight: Leo Choi

Leo Choi, the band's lead guitarist, shares his thoughts on the creative process. "Songwriting for us has always been a collaborative effort. Each of us brings something unique to the table. It's like a puzzle, and every piece matters," he explains. Leo highlights a pivotal moment in their career:

> "The breakthrough hit that changed everything was born out of a jam session. We were just messing around, and suddenly, a melody emerged that felt special. It was magical."

This moment underscores the spontaneity and chemistry that fuels Kompany's music.

Drummer's Reflection: Samir Patel

Samir Patel, the dynamic drummer, discusses the challenges the band faced during their rise to fame. "The pressure can be overwhelming at times. You're constantly trying to meet expectations while staying true to your art," he admits. Samir recalls a particularly tough tour:

> "We had a string of sold-out shows, but I remember feeling exhausted. It was during those moments that we had to lean on each other. Communication was key. We had to remind ourselves why we started this journey in the first place."

Samir's insights reveal the importance of teamwork and support in navigating the complexities of fame.

Bassist's Thoughts: Nia Torres

Nia Torres, the band's bassist, shares her perspective on the evolution of Kompany's sound. "As we grew, so did our music. We experimented with different genres and sounds, and it was liberating," she reflects. Nia emphasizes the role of their fans in this evolution:

> "Our fans have always been our guiding light. They inspire us to push boundaries and explore new horizons. Every time we release something new, it's like sharing a piece of ourselves with them."

Nia's words encapsulate the symbiotic relationship between the band and its audience.

Keyboardist's Insight: Alex Yu

Alex Yu, the keyboardist, offers a unique angle on the band's artistic vision. "Music is a reflection of our experiences. Each album tells a story, and we're constantly evolving," he explains. Alex highlights the importance of reinvention:

> "After our hiatus, we came back with a fresh perspective. It was a chance to rediscover our passion and bring something new to the table. Our latest album is a testament to that growth."

His insights emphasize the significance of reinvention in maintaining artistic relevance.

Looking Ahead: The Band's Vision

As a collective, the members of Kompany share a unified vision for the future. "We want to keep pushing ourselves creatively," they state. "Our journey is far from over, and we're excited to explore new musical territories." This forward-looking perspective reflects their commitment to growth and innovation in the music industry.

In conclusion, the exclusive insights from the band members of Kompany reveal the depth of their artistic journey. Through challenges, triumphs, and personal reflections, they continue to inspire not only each other but also their fans around the world. Their story is a testament to the power of music as a unifying force, and their legacy is one of passion, resilience, and creativity.

Testimonials from collaborators and industry professionals

The journey of Kompany has been marked by collaborations that not only enriched their sound but also forged lasting relationships within the music industry. Here, we present heartfelt testimonials from various collaborators and industry professionals who have witnessed the evolution of Kompany from the frontlines.

> "Working with Kompany was like a breath of fresh air. Their passion for music is infectious, and their creativity knows no bounds. I remember the first time we sat down to write together; it was as if we were all on the same wavelength. They have this unique ability to blend genres while staying true to their roots."
>
> — Liam Carter, Music Producer

ADDITIONAL INTERVIEWS AND QUOTES

Liam Carter, a prominent music producer, played a pivotal role in the production of Kompany's debut album. His insight into their creative process highlights the band's commitment to innovation.

> "Kompany has a sound that resonates with people of all ages. Their lyrics tell stories that are relatable and poignant. I had the pleasure of collaborating on a track for their second album, and I was blown away by their ability to weave personal experiences into universal themes."
> — **Sophie Lin, Singer-Songwriter**

Sophie Lin, an acclaimed singer-songwriter, emphasizes the lyrical depth that Kompany brings to their music. This ability to connect with listeners on a personal level is a hallmark of their artistry.

> "I've seen many bands come and go, but Kompany has something special. Their live performances are electric, and you can feel the energy in the room. They have a way of engaging the audience that makes every show memorable. It's a testament to their hard work and dedication."
> — **Jordan Mitchell, Concert Promoter**

Concert promoter Jordan Mitchell reflects on the band's live performances, which have become a significant aspect of their identity. The connection they foster with their audience is a crucial element of their success.

> "Kompany's music is a fusion of styles that transcends boundaries. Their willingness to experiment and take risks has set them apart in a saturated market. I admire their authenticity and the way they stay true to themselves while pushing the envelope."
> — **Emily Tran, Music Journalist**

Music journalist Emily Tran highlights the innovative spirit of Kompany. Their ability to blend various musical influences while maintaining authenticity is a key factor in their lasting appeal.

> "The first time I heard Kompany's music, I knew they were destined for greatness. Their sound is fresh yet nostalgic, and it has the power to evoke deep emotions. Collaborating with them was one of the highlights of my career."
> — **Michael Reyes, Grammy Award-Winning Producer**

Michael Reyes, a Grammy-winning producer, speaks to the emotional resonance of Kompany's music. His experience underscores the band's capacity to create impactful art that leaves a mark on listeners.

> "Kompany is more than just a band; they are a movement. Their commitment to social issues and philanthropy through music is inspiring. They remind us that art can be a powerful tool for change."
> — Rachel Adams, Philanthropist and Activist

Philanthropist Rachel Adams acknowledges Kompany's dedication to using their platform for positive change. Their activism and commitment to social issues resonate deeply with fans and fellow artists alike.

> "As a fellow musician, I admire how Kompany navigates the complexities of the industry. They have faced challenges that would have broken lesser bands, yet they continue to rise and inspire. It's a privilege to call them friends."
> — David Wong, Indie Artist

Indie artist David Wong speaks to the resilience of Kompany. Their journey through the ups and downs of the music industry serves as an inspiration to many aspiring musicians.

These testimonials reflect the profound impact Kompany has had on those who have collaborated with them. Their journey is not just about music; it's about creating connections, inspiring change, and leaving a lasting legacy in the hearts of fans and fellow artists alike.

Kompany's Top Ten Songs

Fan favorites and critical successes

Kompany has carved a unique niche in the music industry, captivating audiences with their distinctive sound and emotional depth. Among their discography, certain tracks have emerged as fan favorites and critical successes, resonating deeply with listeners and garnering acclaim from music critics alike. This section explores these standout songs, delving into the elements that contributed to their popularity and success.

Defining Fan Favorites

Fan favorites are typically characterized by their widespread appeal, often highlighted by significant streaming numbers, concert sing-alongs, and social media buzz. These tracks often encapsulate the essence of the band's identity, showcasing their musical style and lyrical prowess.

$$\text{Popularity Index} = \frac{\text{Streaming Count} + \text{Radio Play} + \text{Social Media Mentions}}{\text{Time Since Release}} \quad (73)$$

Using the above formula, we can quantify the popularity of Kompany's tracks. For instance, their single *"Echoes of Tomorrow"* has received over 50 million streams, extensive radio play, and has been mentioned thousands of times across social media platforms. This track serves as a quintessential example of how Kompany connects with their audience on a personal level.

Critical Acclaim

Critical success often stems from the combination of innovative sound, lyrical depth, and production quality. Music critics frequently evaluate songs based on their originality, emotional impact, and technical execution. Kompany's *"Whispers in the Wind"* is a prime example, receiving rave reviews for its haunting melody and poignant lyrics that explore themes of love and loss.

$$\text{Critical Success Score} = \frac{\text{Review Scores} + \text{Awards Won}}{\text{Number of Reviews}} \quad (74)$$

Applying this formula, *"Whispers in the Wind"* achieved an average review score of 9.2/10 across 20 publications and won the prestigious *Best Ballad Award* at the National Music Awards, yielding a high Critical Success Score.

Top Fan Favorites and Critical Successes

Here, we highlight some of the most beloved tracks from Kompany's discography, showcasing their journey through music.

- **"Echoes of Tomorrow"**
    - *Release Date:* January 15, 2018
    - *Key Features:* Uplifting chorus, relatable lyrics about hope and perseverance.

- *Achievements:* Over 50 million streams, charted in the top 10 for 12 weeks.

- **"Whispers in the Wind"**

    - *Release Date:* March 22, 2019

    - *Key Features:* Emotional ballad with intricate harmonies and profound lyrics.

    - *Achievements:* Average review score of 9.2, winner of the Best Ballad Award.

- **"Chasing Stars"**

    - *Release Date:* July 10, 2020

    - *Key Features:* Upbeat tempo, infectious melody, and themes of adventure.

    - *Achievements:* Nominated for Best Pop Song, received over 30 million streams.

- **"Fading Light"**

    - *Release Date:* November 5, 2021

    - *Key Features:* Soulful instrumentation, deep lyrical content exploring existential themes.

    - *Achievements:* Critically acclaimed, with a score of 9.0/10 from major music critics.

Cultural Impact

Kompany's music transcends mere entertainment; it has sparked conversations and inspired movements within their fanbase. The lyrics of *"Echoes of Tomorrow"* have been used in various motivational campaigns, while *"Whispers in the Wind"* has been featured in documentaries addressing mental health awareness. This illustrates the profound impact that their music has on listeners, solidifying their place in the cultural zeitgeist.

Conclusion

In summary, the fan favorites and critical successes of Kompany not only highlight their musical talent but also their ability to connect with audiences on multiple levels. As they continue to evolve and innovate, these tracks will remain cornerstones of their legacy, cherished by fans and celebrated by critics for years to come.

A curated list of Kompany's most iconic songs

Kompany's journey through the music industry has been marked by a collection of songs that resonate deeply with fans and critics alike. Each track not only showcases the band's evolution but also captures the essence of their artistic spirit. Below is a curated list of Kompany's most iconic songs, accompanied by insights into their significance and impact.

1. **"Heartbeat"**
   - *Release Year:* 2015
   - *Album: Rhythms of Life*
   - *Overview:* This debut single encapsulated the raw emotion of youthful love and longing. The infectious melody and heartfelt lyrics quickly made it a fan favorite, propelling Kompany into the limelight.
   - *Impact:* "Heartbeat" topped local charts for several weeks and became the anthem for many young couples, solidifying Kompany's place in the local music scene.

2. **"Chasing Shadows"**
   - *Release Year:* 2017
   - *Album: Echoes of Tomorrow*
   - *Overview:* This track marked a significant shift in Kompany's sound, blending electronic elements with their signature acoustic style. The lyrics explore themes of self-discovery and the pursuit of dreams.
   - *Impact:* "Chasing Shadows" received critical acclaim, earning them their first major award and a nomination for Best New Artist at the National Music Awards.

3. **"Rise Up"**
   - *Release Year:* 2019

- *Album: Resilience*
- *Overview:* Written during a tumultuous period for the band, "Rise Up" serves as a powerful anthem of perseverance and hope. The song's uplifting chorus encourages listeners to overcome adversity.
- *Impact:* This song became synonymous with empowerment movements and was featured in various charitable campaigns, further expanding Kompany's influence beyond music.

4. **"Echoes of the Past"**

   - *Release Year:* 2021
   - *Album: Reflections*
   - *Overview:* A poignant ballad that reflects on nostalgia and the bittersweet nature of memories. The song showcases the band's lyrical depth and emotional range, resonating with fans of all ages.
   - *Impact:* "Echoes of the Past" garnered significant radio play and sparked conversations about the importance of cherishing memories, making it a staple in Kompany's live performances.

5. **"Together We Stand"**

   - *Release Year:* 2023
   - *Album: Unity*
   - *Overview:* This recent release embodies the spirit of community and solidarity, especially in the wake of global challenges. The collaborative nature of the song features guest artists from various genres, showcasing Kompany's versatility.
   - *Impact:* "Together We Stand" quickly became an anthem for social movements and was lauded for its message of unity, earning praise from both fans and critics for its timely relevance.

Conclusion: Each of these songs represents a milestone in Kompany's career, reflecting their growth as artists and their ability to connect with listeners on a profound level. From the early days of "Heartbeat" to the anthemic "Together We Stand," Kompany continues to inspire and uplift, leaving an indelible mark on the music landscape.

Note: For further exploration of Kompany's discography, refer to the Appendix section for a complete list of albums, singles, and notable collaborations.

Resources and Recommended Reading

Other books and articles about Kompany

In the ever-evolving landscape of music literature, the story of Kompany has inspired a myriad of authors, journalists, and music enthusiasts to delve deeper into their journey. Below are some notable works that explore the band's impact, evolution, and cultural significance.

Books

- **Kompany: The Sound of a Generation** by Laura Voss. This biography offers an in-depth look at the band's formation and rise to fame, highlighting key moments that shaped their musical identity. Voss interviews band members, producers, and fans, providing a multifaceted perspective on their journey.

- **Echoes of Kompany: A Musical Legacy** by Jonathan Reed. This book analyzes the musical styles and influences that have permeated Kompany's discography. Reed breaks down their major albums track by track, discussing the lyrical themes and production techniques that define their sound.

- **Kompany Unplugged: Behind the Scenes** by Sarah Mitchell. A behind-the-scenes account of the band's tours, this book captures the essence of live performances and the connection between the band and their fans. Mitchell includes anecdotes from tour crew and fans, illustrating the emotional highs and lows of life on the road.

Articles

- "**The Rise of Kompany: From Local Heroes to Global Icons**" by Mark Thompson, published in *Music Today*. This article traces the trajectory of Kompany's career, focusing on their breakthrough moments and the strategies they employed to gain national and international recognition.

- "**Kompany's Creative Evolution: A Study of Their Musical Journey**" by Emily Chen, featured in *The Journal of Contemporary Music*. Chen provides an analytical perspective on the band's evolution over the years, examining their shifts in style and the influences that have shaped their artistic direction.

- "The Heart of Kompany: Fan Culture and Community" by David Klein, published in *Cultural Studies Quarterly*. This article explores the relationship between Kompany and their fanbase, discussing how their music has fostered a sense of community and belonging among listeners.

Online Resources

The digital age has also seen a plethora of online content dedicated to Kompany. Various blogs, podcasts, and fan sites have emerged, offering analyses, reviews, and discussions about the band's work.

- **Kompany Fan Blog** - A dedicated space for fans to share their thoughts, experiences, and creative interpretations of the band's music. The blog features interviews with fans and covers recent news and events related to the band.

- **The Kompany Podcast** - Hosted by music enthusiasts, this podcast delves into the band's discography, exploring each album's themes and the stories behind the songs. Episodes often feature guest appearances from music critics and industry insiders.

- **Kompany Wiki** - An extensive online encyclopedia that documents the band's history, discography, and significant events. The wiki is constantly updated by fans and serves as a comprehensive resource for anyone looking to learn more about Kompany.

Conclusion

The literature surrounding Kompany not only highlights their musical achievements but also reflects their cultural impact and the profound connection they share with their fans. As new generations discover their music, it is likely that more works will emerge, further enriching the narrative of this remarkable band.

Further exploration of the band's history and impact

Kompany's journey through the music industry is not just a tale of success; it is a profound narrative that encapsulates the evolution of a band that has resonated deeply with its audience. To fully appreciate the impact of Kompany, we must delve into various dimensions of their history, examining the socio-cultural context in which they emerged, their musical innovations, and the broader implications of their work.

Cultural Context and Emergence

The late 2000s and early 2010s marked a significant shift in the music industry, characterized by the rise of digital platforms and the decline of traditional record sales. This era saw an influx of new genres and a blending of musical styles, creating a fertile ground for bands like Kompany to thrive. Their formation as childhood friends with a shared passion for music positioned them uniquely to capture the zeitgeist of this transitional period.

The socio-political landscape during this time also played a crucial role. Issues such as climate change, social justice, and mental health began to surface in public discourse, influencing the themes and messages conveyed through music. Kompany's ability to weave these themes into their lyrics not only resonated with fans but also positioned them as a voice for a generation seeking authenticity and connection.

Musical Innovations

Kompany's sound is a fusion of various genres, including pop, rock, and electronic music, which reflects their diverse influences and experiences. This eclectic style has allowed them to appeal to a wide audience while maintaining a unique identity.

$$f(x) = a \cdot \sin(bx + c) + d \qquad (75)$$

In this equation, $f(x)$ represents the band's sound, where a, b, c, and d symbolize the various influences that shape their music, such as lyrical content, instrumentation, and production techniques. The oscillation of the sine function illustrates how their sound evolves over time, adapting to trends while remaining true to their roots.

One of the band's significant innovations was their approach to songwriting. They often collaborated with emerging artists and producers, which not only enriched their sound but also fostered a sense of community within the music industry. This collaborative spirit is evident in their hit singles, which often feature guest artists who bring fresh perspectives and styles.

Broader Implications of Their Work

Kompany's influence extends beyond their music; they have become cultural icons, inspiring a new generation of musicians and fans. Their commitment to authenticity and vulnerability in their lyrics has encouraged many to embrace their own stories and struggles. This cultural shift is particularly significant in an age where mental health is increasingly recognized as a vital aspect of overall well-being.

The band's philanthropic efforts further amplify their impact. By using their platform to support various charitable causes, they have demonstrated that music can be a powerful tool for change. Their involvement in campaigns addressing issues such as homelessness, education, and environmental sustainability has not only raised awareness but has also mobilized their fan base to take action.

Legacy and Future Exploration

As we reflect on Kompany's journey, it is essential to consider the legacy they are building. Their ability to adapt to changing musical landscapes while staying true to their core values is a testament to their resilience and vision.

In exploring their future impact, we must consider the following questions:

- How will Kompany continue to innovate musically in an ever-evolving industry?
- In what ways can they further engage with their audience on social issues?
- What role will technology play in shaping their future sound and reach?

These questions invite a deeper exploration of not only Kompany's trajectory but also the broader music industry landscape. As they continue to evolve, their story will undoubtedly inspire future musicians to carve their paths, encouraging a culture of creativity and social responsibility.

In conclusion, the exploration of Kompany's history and impact reveals a complex interplay of cultural context, musical innovation, and social responsibility. Their journey serves as a case study for understanding the transformative power of music and its ability to connect, inspire, and effect change in society.

About the Author

Mei Raj's personal connection to Kompany

As a devoted follower of Kompany since their inception, my connection to the band transcends mere fandom; it is deeply woven into the fabric of my own musical journey. My first encounter with their music was during a local festival where they performed an electrifying set that resonated with my youthful aspirations. The raw emotion and authenticity in their sound ignited a spark within me, compelling me to explore my own musical identity.

Growing up in a town not far from theirs, I witnessed firsthand the evolution of Kompany from a group of childhood friends to a formidable force in the music

ABOUT THE AUTHOR

industry. Their story mirrored my own experiences—filled with dreams, struggles, and the relentless pursuit of passion. This proximity allowed me to cultivate a personal admiration for each member, as I saw them not just as artists, but as individuals navigating the complexities of life and creativity.

In my early years, I often found solace in their lyrics, which spoke of love, loss, and the trials of growing up. Their songs became the soundtrack to my teenage years, capturing moments of joy and heartbreak alike. The relatability of their music fostered a sense of connection that felt almost intimate, as if they were articulating my own emotions and experiences.

Moreover, my journey as a writer has been significantly influenced by Kompany's lyrical storytelling. The way they weave narratives into their songs has taught me the power of words and the importance of vulnerability in art. I often reflect on the theory of *narrative transportation*, which posits that individuals can become emotionally involved in stories, leading to changes in beliefs and attitudes. This theory resonates with my experiences as a listener, as Kompany's music has shaped my perspectives and inspired my creative endeavors.

In my role as a biographer, I have sought to capture the essence of Kompany's journey, delving into the intricacies of their artistic process and the challenges they faced along the way. This task has not only deepened my appreciation for their work but has also allowed me to contribute to the narrative of a band that has significantly impacted my life.

One particular instance stands out in my memory: attending a small, intimate concert where the band performed an acoustic set. The vulnerability displayed by the members as they shared personal stories between songs was profound. It was a reminder of the human experience behind the music, highlighting the importance of connection and community. This experience crystallized my belief in the transformative power of music, and it is a theme I strive to convey in this biography.

As I pen these words, I am reminded of the challenges I faced in my own writing journey—self-doubt, fear of failure, and the relentless pursuit of authenticity. These struggles are not unlike those experienced by Kompany as they navigated the tumultuous waters of fame and artistry. Their resilience serves as a beacon of hope, inspiring me to persist in my creative endeavors.

In conclusion, my personal connection to Kompany is a testament to the profound impact that music can have on our lives. It is a bond forged through shared experiences, emotional resonance, and a mutual love for creativity. As I reflect on their journey, I am filled with gratitude for the inspiration they have provided, and I am honored to share their story with the world.

Other works by Mei Raj

Mei Raj, an author and musician, has crafted several notable works that explore the intersection of music, culture, and personal experience. Her writing often reflects the emotional depth and storytelling prowess seen in her music, resonating with readers and fans alike. Below is a selection of her other works that highlight her versatility and passion for the arts.

Echoes of the Heart: A Memoir

In this intimate memoir, Mei Raj delves into her personal journey as an artist, sharing the struggles and triumphs that shaped her career. The book is structured around pivotal moments in her life, using lyrical prose to evoke the emotions tied to each experience. Readers are taken on a journey through her childhood, the challenges of breaking into the music industry, and the relationships that influenced her art.

Harmonies of Change: Music and Social Justice

This thought-provoking work examines the role of music in social movements, highlighting how artists have used their platforms to advocate for change. Mei Raj combines research with personal anecdotes, illustrating the power of music as a tool for activism. The book includes case studies of influential musicians and their contributions to various causes, making a compelling argument for the importance of artistic expression in societal progress.

The Soundtrack of Our Lives: A Collection of Essays

In this collection, Mei Raj presents a series of essays that reflect on the impact of music on personal identity and cultural narratives. Each essay explores different genres and their significance in shaping societal views. Through her keen observations and personal reflections, Mei Raj invites readers to consider how music serves as a backdrop to their own life stories.

Melodies of Memory: A Children's Book

Targeted at younger audiences, this beautifully illustrated children's book introduces the joys of music through engaging stories and vibrant imagery. Mei Raj weaves tales of adventure and friendship, each accompanied by a musical theme that encourages children to explore their creativity. The book aims to inspire a love of music in the next generation, fostering an appreciation for the arts.

ABOUT THE AUTHOR

Rhythms of the World: A Global Exploration of Music

In this expansive work, Mei Raj takes readers on a journey across continents, exploring the diverse musical traditions that exist around the globe. The book is a celebration of cultural diversity, showcasing how music reflects the values, histories, and experiences of different communities. Through in-depth interviews with musicians and ethnographic research, Mei Raj highlights the universal language of music and its ability to connect people from all walks of life.

Songwriting Secrets: Crafting Your Musical Voice

This practical guide for aspiring songwriters offers insights into the creative process behind crafting memorable songs. Mei Raj shares her personal techniques, including lyrical composition, melody creation, and the importance of storytelling in songwriting. The book includes exercises and prompts designed to help readers unlock their creativity and develop their unique musical voices.

The Art of Collaboration: Working with Other Musicians

In this insightful exploration of collaboration in the music industry, Mei Raj discusses the dynamics of working with other artists. She shares her experiences of collaborating with various musicians, highlighting the joys and challenges that come with creative partnerships. The book provides practical advice on how to navigate differences in artistic vision while fostering a spirit of cooperation and mutual respect.

Voices of Resilience: Stories from the Music Industry

This anthology features stories from a diverse group of musicians who have faced adversity in their careers. Mei Raj curates these narratives, showcasing the resilience and determination of artists who have overcome obstacles to achieve their dreams. The book serves as a testament to the power of perseverance and the unbreakable spirit of those who pursue their passion for music.

Through these works, Mei Raj continues to inspire and engage audiences, blending her love for music with her talent for storytelling. Each publication reflects her dedication to the arts and her desire to connect with readers on a profound level, ensuring that her voice resonates beyond the stage.

Contact information for the author

For inquiries, collaborations, or feedback regarding this biography or any other works by the author, please reach out through the following channels:

- Email: mei.raj.author@example.com
- Website: www.meirajmusic.com
- Social Media:
  - Twitter: https://twitter.com/meirajmusic
  - Instagram: https://instagram.com/meirajmusic
  - Facebook: https://facebook.com/meirajmusic
  - LinkedIn: https://linkedin.com/in/meirajmusic

For those interested in a deeper dive into the creative process and the journey of Kompany, Mei Raj welcomes discussions and engagement with fans, music enthusiasts, and fellow authors.

Media Inquiries: For media-related questions, interviews, or promotional events, please contact the public relations team at:

- Email: press@meirajmusic.com
- Phone: +1 (555) 123-4567

Booking Information: For booking events, speaking engagements, or performances, please reach out to the booking agent at:

- Email: bookings@meirajmusic.com
- Phone: +1 (555) 987-6543

Mei Raj values the connection with readers and fans, and is eager to hear your thoughts, stories, and experiences related to Kompany's music and impact. Your feedback is important and helps shape future works and projects.

Newsletter Subscription: To stay updated on new releases, events, and exclusive content, consider subscribing to the monthly newsletter via the website. Subscribers will receive behind-the-scenes insights, early access to new works, and special offers.

Thank you for your interest in Mei Raj and the story of Kompany. Your support means the world, and together, we can continue to celebrate the magic of music and the connections it fosters.

Mailing Address: For physical correspondence, fan mail, or gifts, please send to:

ABOUT THE AUTHOR

Mei Raj
P.O. Box 12345
Music City, CA 90210
USA

Please allow time for responses, as the author is often engaged in various projects and commitments. However, each message is cherished, and efforts will be made to reply as soon as possible.

Thank you for being a part of this journey, and for your continued support of Kompany and its music. Together, let's keep the rhythm alive!

Index

-doubt, 2, 4, 6, 10, 11, 48

a, 1–7, 9–16, 19–23, 25–28, 30–37, 39, 41–43, 45–53, 55–59, 61–87, 89, 91–97, 99–107, 109–118, 120–124, 126–130, 135, 138–148, 150–152, 155, 157–164
ability, 13, 23, 45, 47, 48, 69, 72, 74, 102–104, 114, 118, 120, 122, 123, 140, 143, 147, 151, 155, 159, 160, 163
acceptance, 60
access, 20
acclaim, 152
accolade, 122, 126
achievement, 37, 145
achieving, 34, 60, 73
acknowledgment, 121
acoustic, 22, 48, 55, 80, 147, 161
act, 1, 6, 73
action, 33, 92, 111, 116, 160
activism, 92, 97, 105–107, 110, 111, 152, 162
adaptability, 56, 66, 69, 114
addition, 22, 86, 100, 122, 147
address, 13, 31, 52, 76, 79

admiration, 20, 62
adolescence, 1
adrenaline, 48
advantage, 79
adversity, 71, 77, 163
advice, 163
advocacy, 107
advocate, 13, 105, 110, 117, 147, 162
age, 6, 20, 106, 158, 159
air, 47
album, 13, 23, 27, 28, 30, 31, 44, 53, 55, 62, 68, 71–73, 84, 92, 93, 99, 123, 135, 138, 151
Alex Thompson, 146, 147
Alex Turner, 94
allure, 76
along, 21, 126, 128, 143, 161
anthem, 22, 116
anthology, 163
anticipation, 11
anxiety, 13, 28, 47, 48, 78, 96, 147
appeal, 36, 59, 68, 114, 151, 153, 159
appetite, 75
applause, 6
appreciation, 52, 84, 87, 127, 161
approach, 4, 13, 15, 23, 26, 31, 32,

34, 47, 51, 52, 55, 58, 73, 76, 81, 102, 106, 111, 114, 117, 142, 159
area, 21
argument, 68, 162
arrangement, 34, 63, 68, 73
array, 3, 62, 101
art, 27, 111, 118, 148, 152, 162
article, 12
artist, 6, 23, 27, 51, 61, 63, 112, 147, 152, 162
artistry, 48, 49, 87, 97, 102, 131, 147, 151
aspect, 47, 48, 79, 81, 121, 151, 159
assortment, 5
atmosphere, 15, 27, 37, 48, 51, 55, 73
attention, 11, 12, 15, 21, 22, 43, 76, 77, 112, 147
audience, 6, 10, 11, 15, 16, 20, 23, 25, 30, 34, 37, 47, 48, 51, 52, 56, 62–64, 66, 68, 76, 77, 81, 87, 102, 103, 113, 116, 121, 127, 140, 147–149, 151, 158, 159
authenticity, 5, 10, 11, 14, 20, 21, 36, 47, 64, 84, 97, 99, 102, 107, 114, 120, 148, 151, 159, 160
author, 162, 164, 165
award, 59, 126
awareness, 92, 106, 117, 147, 160
awkwardness, 1

backdrop, 162
backing, 42
balance, 36, 43, 59, 62, 70, 73
balancing, 59, 73

band, 1–7, 9–16, 19–22, 25–27, 30–32, 34, 36, 37, 39, 43, 45–49, 51–54, 56–58, 61, 64–85, 87, 89, 91–97, 99–102, 105, 107, 110, 116–118, 120–122, 126, 127, 143, 145–153, 155, 157–161
bandmate, 58
base, 14, 19–22, 43, 60, 96, 118, 120, 140, 143, 147, 160
bassist, 83, 147
beacon, 99, 116
beat, 17
beauty, 83, 140, 143
bedrock, 72
beginning, 20, 36, 37, 89, 143
being, 2, 32, 39, 42, 49, 52, 58, 68, 73, 76, 83, 147, 159
belief, 2, 6, 109, 117, 128, 161
belonging, 4, 15, 48, 92, 106, 109
benefit, 13, 31
betrayal, 76
biographer, 161
biography, 161, 164
birth, 6, 7
blend, 5, 13, 16, 22, 25, 30, 31, 47, 64, 100, 103, 117, 123, 151
blending, 14, 23, 26, 62, 63, 94, 102, 141, 159, 163
block, 27
body, 30
bond, 1, 2, 5, 10, 13, 16, 20, 31, 37, 52, 58, 70, 73, 74, 77, 80, 87, 96, 147, 161
book, 162, 163
brainstorming, 25, 31, 65, 93
brand, 15, 45, 113
break, 16, 58, 83, 84

Index 169

breakdown, 13
breakout, 116
breakthrough, 46, 126
breakup, 75, 77, 79, 93
breathing, 48
bridge, 57
Brink, 76
building, 7, 16, 20, 21, 39, 160
burnout, 52
buzz, 35, 76, 153
byproduct, 19, 120

cacophony, 3
call, 33
camaraderie, 3, 6, 79, 87, 92
campaign, 34, 92
capacity, 152
care, 32, 39, 58, 59, 83, 147
career, 2, 17, 22, 31, 41, 43, 49, 63, 100, 107, 120, 122–124, 138, 140, 143, 145, 162
case, 55, 67, 75, 77, 81, 160, 162
catalyst, 22, 62, 71, 89, 105
catharsis, 48
celebration, 48, 49, 96, 123, 126, 163
celebrity, 76
certificate, 61
challenge, 14, 21, 33, 36, 39, 52, 87, 104, 116, 147
change, 33, 97, 104, 105, 107, 110, 111, 116, 117, 122, 130, 139, 145, 152, 159, 160, 162
channel, 84
chaos, 58, 82, 94
chapter, 6, 30, 37, 43, 49, 77, 84, 87, 89, 138
chart, 34, 43, 45, 51, 94, 111, 114, 121, 139

check, 32
cheer, 48, 127
chemistry, 3, 86
childhood, 1, 5, 9, 10, 13, 101, 143, 159, 162
choice, 64
chord, 25
chorus, 33, 116
chronicle, 95, 146
clap, 48
clarity, 84
clash, 63
classic, 2, 9, 62
climate, 116, 159
closeness, 13
club, 48
co, 63
collaboration, 2, 3, 12, 13, 16, 17, 22, 23, 25, 27, 31, 43, 46, 56, 62–64, 66, 73, 82, 87, 94, 99, 100, 112, 117, 128, 139–143, 163
collection, 138, 155, 162
collective, 6, 25, 32, 37, 48, 51, 57, 61, 70, 71, 73, 83, 87, 92, 93, 97, 99, 111, 116, 126, 146, 148
collide, 50, 54
combination, 75
comeback, 93
comfort, 93
commentary, 116
commercialism, 99
commitment, 6, 10, 12, 21, 33, 37, 43, 47, 52, 69, 71, 76, 79, 84, 92, 96, 97, 99, 102, 104, 105, 107, 109, 111, 114, 117, 118, 122, 128,

138, 139, 141, 145, 147, 148, 151, 152, 159
communication, 13, 14, 21, 23, 43, 56, 59, 71–74, 77–79, 83, 84, 96, 111
community, 3, 4, 11, 12, 14–17, 23, 31, 37, 49, 52, 66, 77, 93, 96, 99, 107, 109–111, 114, 117, 118, 120, 124, 128, 143, 147, 148, 159, 161
compassion, 109
competition, 11, 15
component, 71
composite, 121
composition, 34, 81, 163
compromise, 2, 9, 13, 14, 23, 62, 72–74, 83, 96
concept, 46, 73
concert, 20, 93, 105, 153, 161
conclusion, 10, 21, 39, 49, 50, 52, 54, 56, 59, 74, 77, 84, 93, 97, 102, 107, 111, 116, 118, 120, 124, 126, 129, 130, 140, 145, 148, 150, 160, 161
conduit, 37
conference, 79
confidence, 146
conflict, 14, 23, 55, 68
connection, 10, 17, 20, 21, 23, 27, 39, 47–49, 51, 76, 80, 87, 91, 95, 97, 112, 116, 127, 130, 140, 151, 158–161, 164
consciousness, 129
conservation, 117
consideration, 63
contemporary, 5, 9, 62, 103
content, 20, 23, 63, 106, 158

contest, 146
context, 67, 73, 74, 76, 120, 158, 160
contract, 42
contribution, 13, 121
control, 78
convergence, 9
cooperation, 163
core, 81, 160
cornerstone, 49, 52, 109, 110, 148
country, 147
countryside, 81
craft, 3, 11, 12, 14, 37, 63, 77, 79, 93, 96, 102, 127, 146–148
creation, 2, 23, 52, 62, 163
creative, 1, 4, 13, 21, 23, 27, 30, 39, 42, 43, 49, 52–56, 61, 63–67, 69, 71–74, 78, 79, 82, 83, 87, 89, 102, 116, 143, 147, 151, 163, 164
creativity, 14, 16, 22, 25, 27, 29, 30, 37, 47, 53, 55, 62, 69, 72, 84, 85, 87, 95–97, 99, 116, 117, 127, 142, 143, 145, 148, 150, 160, 161, 163
cross, 142
crowd, 47, 96
crucible, 69
cry, 116
culmination, 6, 12, 99, 126
culture, 15, 76, 116, 117, 160, 162
cycle, 47

damage, 47
dance, 48
darkness, 48
David Wong, 152
day, 2
debut, 31, 53, 99, 151
decision, 27, 32, 41, 83

Index

decline, 159
dedication, 6, 59, 77, 92, 97, 102, 109, 112, 115, 117, 122, 128, 152, 163
delay, 34
deliberation, 6, 83
demographic, 112
departure, 23, 62
depth, 102, 150–152, 162, 163
desire, 10, 72, 84, 107, 163
despair, 32
destination, 127
determination, 11, 14, 163
development, 23, 46, 67, 71, 101
devotion, 92
dialogue, 74, 83, 111, 143
difference, 107, 111, 122
direction, 2, 13, 71–73, 78
disagreement, 6, 68, 78
disappointment, 21
disaster, 71
disbandment, 78, 93
discography, 117, 135, 141, 152, 153
disconnection, 39
discord, 56, 67, 75
discourse, 75, 76, 159
discovery, 26, 70, 97, 99, 102
discussion, 73
display, 76
dissemination, 113
Dissonance, 100
distribution, 46
distrust, 78
dive, 26, 164
divergence, 9, 55, 72
diversity, 64, 103, 117, 142, 163
divide, 78
doubt, 2, 4, 6, 10, 11, 48, 96
downtime, 57

drama, 75
dream, 2, 6, 7, 99, 127
driving, 11, 34, 109, 117
drumbeat, 34
drummer, 3, 83, 147
dynamic, 1, 116, 145

echo, 111, 140
editing, 46
edition, 20
education, 83, 160
effect, 107, 160
effectiveness, 77
effort, 51, 61, 65, 81, 116, 126
Einstein, 1
element, 112, 151
eligibility, 59
Emily Tran, 151
emotion, 99, 116, 160
encore, 39
encounter, 6, 160
encouragement, 87, 127
end, 43, 80
endeavor, 19, 21, 54, 147
energy, 1, 10, 20, 37, 47, 48, 52, 96, 127
engagement, 15, 16, 19–21, 35, 37, 51, 52, 77, 93, 107, 120, 121, 148, 164
entertainment, 76, 105, 116
enthusiasm, 1, 93
entry, 14
environment, 25, 32, 53, 56, 74, 76, 78, 79, 83, 97, 101, 111, 128
epiphany, 11
equation, 1, 4, 5, 7, 13, 20, 21, 31, 32, 36, 53, 57, 58, 61, 73, 75, 77, 102, 103, 105, 112,

113, 115, 121, 122, 127, 128, 142
equipment, 31
era, 105, 159
escape, 83
essay, 162
essence, 14, 36, 81, 85, 94, 95, 121, 122, 127, 138, 142, 153, 155, 161
estate, 75
ethos, 114
evening, 6
event, 145
evolution, 43, 47, 54, 62, 66, 95, 97, 117, 118, 123, 135, 138, 146, 150, 155, 157, 158
example, 13, 23, 47, 57, 63, 72, 76, 81, 83, 92, 99, 112, 115, 146
excellence, 121, 122
exception, 70
excitement, 11, 28, 37, 47
exclusivity, 21
expectation, 53
experience, 3, 6, 12, 23, 27, 43, 48, 49, 51, 56, 61, 76, 80, 81, 84, 99, 126, 131, 152, 161, 162
experimentation, 3, 10, 14, 25, 96, 99, 142
expertise, 27, 30, 32, 128
exploration, 10, 25, 27, 64, 71, 80–82, 85, 87, 115, 141, 160, 163
expression, 1, 45, 54, 72, 74, 85, 116, 162

fabric, 5, 102, 122, 160
face, 48, 77, 78, 84, 143
factor, 78, 151
failure, 2
fame, 15, 22, 51–55, 57–59, 64, 69, 72, 74, 77, 78, 82, 96, 105, 110, 116, 147, 149
family, 2, 15, 57, 127, 128
fan, 7, 14, 19–22, 43, 51, 52, 60, 75–77, 92, 93, 96, 118, 120, 121, 140, 143, 147, 152, 155, 158, 160
fanbase, 36, 52, 76, 78, 91, 92, 109
fandom, 118, 160
favorite, 2, 3, 93
fear, 2, 4, 36, 53, 76
feature, 12, 159
feedback, 16, 48, 87, 164
feeling, 53, 58, 76, 78
fellow, 22, 120, 122, 152, 164
fester, 79
festival, 63, 160
filming, 46
finding, 4, 10, 74
firsthand, 57
fitness, 147
flourishing, 85
focus, 52, 79, 81, 128
folk, 3, 9, 14, 26, 34, 80
follower, 160
following, 13, 14, 21, 32, 34, 53, 75, 77, 102, 113, 118, 120, 160, 164
force, 11, 102, 103, 116, 117, 150
formation, 159
formula, 34, 113
foster, 58, 79, 92, 106, 120, 151
foundation, 1–3, 5, 12, 14, 27, 30, 39, 96, 120
framework, 31
freedom, 43

Index

frenzy, 76, 96
friction, 23, 96
friendship, 2, 6, 7, 10, 96
front, 10
frustration, 10, 32, 72
function, 112
fund, 31
fundraising, 13, 109
fusion, 36, 55, 62, 100, 102, 159
future, 3, 5, 10, 12, 14, 17, 27, 30, 37, 45, 47, 63, 64, 66, 82, 92, 95, 97, 102, 104, 111, 114, 116, 117, 126, 129, 130, 142, 143, 145, 146, 148, 160, 164

garage, 3
gaze, 75, 95
generation, 66, 83, 97, 100, 102, 114, 116, 123, 159
genre, 23, 26, 64, 102, 117, 142
gesture, 93
gig, 11
glass, 76
globe, 99, 123, 129, 163
go, 13
goal, 73
good, 76, 109, 110, 117
gratitude, 126, 127, 147, 161
greet, 52
ground, 5, 74, 159
groundwork, 2, 10
group, 3, 12, 43, 49, 67, 73, 75, 163
growth, 5, 6, 10, 23, 32, 33, 47, 56, 66, 69–71, 74, 97, 123, 135, 140, 142, 143, 146, 148
guest, 23, 141, 159
guidance, 32, 100, 117
guide, 17, 37, 163
guitar, 34, 146
guitarist, 25, 71, 146

hallmark, 102, 151
hand, 11
handful, 11
harmony, 56, 67, 74
head, 39, 47, 79, 80
headline, 78
health, 32, 39, 54, 58, 59, 76, 77, 84, 117, 147, 159
heart, 10, 17, 25, 37, 96, 100
heartbeat, 7, 97, 127, 140
heartbreak, 25, 161
help, 48, 79, 163
hesitation, 128
hiatus, 83
high, 3, 63, 68, 72, 147
highlight, 74, 114, 143, 147, 153, 155, 162
history, 86, 114, 118, 122, 140, 158, 160
hit, 22, 46, 62, 73, 81, 112, 116, 126, 159
homelessness, 160
hometown, 10, 143
honor, 143
hope, 33, 94, 99, 116, 127, 129
horizon, 97
hum, 28
humanity, 50
hurdle, 6, 13, 27, 31

idea, 89
identity, 2, 5, 6, 10, 12, 14, 15, 27, 36, 37, 39, 41, 45, 48–50, 54, 56, 63, 81, 87, 94, 96, 97, 103, 107, 109, 110,

116, 138, 141, 143, 146, 148, 151, 153, 159, 160, 162
image, 57, 77
impact, 21, 27, 30, 34, 37, 39, 41, 43, 46, 49, 52, 76–78, 93, 97, 100, 102–105, 111, 112, 116, 117, 120–122, 126, 135, 138, 139, 142, 144, 148, 152, 155, 157, 158, 160–162, 164
implementation, 39
importance, 3, 6, 12, 14, 16, 23, 32, 43, 52, 56, 59, 60, 71, 72, 74, 77, 82, 84, 87, 97, 111, 117, 120, 121, 147, 149, 161–163
imprint, 116
in, 1–7, 9–17, 19–23, 25, 27, 28, 30, 32, 34, 36, 37, 43, 46–63, 66, 67, 69, 71, 73–84, 86, 87, 89, 92–97, 99–104, 106, 107, 109, 111–114, 117, 120, 122–124, 126–129, 135, 138, 140, 142, 143, 145–147, 149–152, 158–165
inception, 5, 160
incident, 68
inclusivity, 117, 118
incorporation, 55
Indie, 152
individual, 6, 9, 22, 48, 57, 58, 67, 70–73, 81, 83, 85–87, 97, 128, 147, 148
industry, 3, 14, 19, 21, 23, 27, 30, 32, 36, 37, 39, 43, 47, 52, 53, 55, 59, 61–64, 66, 69–71, 82, 84, 89, 92, 93, 97, 99–104, 107, 113, 114, 116–118, 120–123, 135, 140, 142–144, 147, 150, 152, 155, 158–160, 162, 163
influence, 37, 47, 48, 61–64, 97, 102, 104, 105, 110, 111, 120, 122, 129, 144, 159
influx, 159
information, 76, 77
ink, 42
innocence, 1
innovation, 27, 66, 112, 114, 116, 118, 151, 160
ins, 32
insider, 76
insight, 30, 151
inspiration, 5, 6, 9, 26, 27, 30, 34, 51, 66, 81, 87, 89, 93, 99, 109, 116, 148, 152, 161
instance, 3, 9, 13, 23, 25, 39, 46–48, 53, 55, 63, 71, 73, 76, 78–80, 92, 93, 99, 114, 116, 147, 161
instrumentation, 34, 55
integration, 101
integrity, 27, 36, 43, 55, 63, 73, 102
interaction, 20
interest, 164
interplay, 67, 75, 160
intersection, 110, 162
intimacy, 51
intrigue, 75
introspection, 11, 82, 85, 97
investment, 27, 30
involvement, 107, 117, 160
isolation, 78
issue, 21, 27

Index 175

jam, 6, 81, 126
Jamie, 22
Jamie Lee, 146, 147
Jamie Lee, 22
jazz, 3
Jordan Mitchell, 151
journalist, 151
journey, 1, 2, 7, 10, 12, 14–16, 19, 21–23, 25, 27, 30, 36, 37, 41, 45–47, 49, 52, 54, 56, 59, 61, 64, 66, 67, 69–71, 74, 75, 78–80, 82, 87, 89, 91, 93–97, 99, 103, 110–112, 114, 116, 118, 120, 122–124, 126, 127, 129, 130, 138, 140, 141, 143, 145–147, 150, 152, 153, 155, 157, 158, 160–164
joy, 48–50, 81, 161
judgment, 31
justice, 159

key, 46, 59, 63, 81, 151
kind, 49, 92
knowledge, 83, 126, 129

label, 41–43, 53, 92, 144
landscape, 9, 17, 23, 27, 46, 47, 54, 64, 102, 103, 114, 117, 120, 123, 138, 157, 159, 160
language, 114, 128, 163
laughter, 6, 48, 49, 126
layer, 55
lead, 23, 51, 62, 81, 82, 87, 97, 143, 146
learning, 32
leg, 39

legacy, 7, 21, 39, 45, 47, 50, 52, 61, 64, 69, 71, 87, 93, 97, 101, 102, 104, 107, 109, 111, 116–118, 122–124, 126, 127, 129, 130, 140, 143, 145, 148, 150, 152, 155, 160
level, 20, 45, 46, 49, 52, 61, 63, 102, 116, 118, 120, 151, 163
Liam Carter, 151
life, 10, 49, 57, 59, 74, 127, 143, 147, 161–163
lifeline, 91
lifestyle, 147
light, 53, 97
limelight, 123, 126
line, 107
list, 155
listening, 2, 73, 74, 93
literature, 157, 158
live, 10, 20, 21, 35, 37, 39, 47–49, 51, 124, 140, 151
living, 4, 25, 147
London, 114
longevity, 67, 72
longing, 81, 114
look, 97, 126, 148
loop, 48
loss, 26, 102, 161
love, 1, 11, 26, 94, 102, 114, 118, 126, 128, 129, 161, 163
loyalty, 20, 21, 66, 77, 91–93, 96, 120
lyric, 53, 96

machinery, 28
magazine, 12
magic, 49, 50, 64, 143, 164
major, 41–43, 114, 135, 144

making, 5, 25, 37, 81, 100, 111, 162
management, 61, 76, 79
manifestation, 5
mark, 47, 52, 64, 97, 102–104, 107, 118, 129, 152
Mark Rivera, 147
market, 14, 15, 21
marketing, 31, 34, 46, 113
mass, 1
material, 3
meaning, 6
means, 1, 37, 39, 63, 111, 164
measure, 115
media, 12, 20, 21, 35, 36, 45, 47, 52, 66, 75–79, 93, 96, 106, 107, 109, 113, 147, 153
meditation, 84
meet, 52, 92
Mei Raj, 143, 162–164
melody, 65, 163
member, 2–5, 9, 13, 23, 25, 31, 37, 55, 57, 61, 68, 70, 72, 76, 80, 83, 93, 97, 128, 146–148
membership, 20
memoir, 162
memory, 127, 161
mentorship, 32, 100, 104, 106, 118
merchandise, 13, 20, 31
message, 73, 129, 165
metaphor, 1
Mia, 71
mic, 15
Michael Reyes, 152
midst, 36, 70
milestone, 6, 41
mindfulness, 39
misinformation, 77, 79
mission, 107

mix, 2, 11, 28, 34, 101
model, 13, 107
moment, 5, 6, 10, 11, 37, 41, 43, 47, 48, 61, 64, 82, 122, 123, 126, 127
momentum, 55
montage, 93
morale, 92
move, 130
movement, 66
music, 1–7, 10–17, 19–23, 25, 27, 30, 33, 36, 37, 39, 41, 43, 45–50, 52–54, 59, 61, 62, 64, 66, 67, 69–72, 74, 76, 77, 79–84, 89, 92–94, 96, 97, 99–105, 107, 109–114, 116–118, 120–124, 126–130, 135, 138–148, 150–153, 155, 157–164
musicality, 135
musician, 7, 22, 162
myriad, 4, 5, 14, 30, 43, 69, 157
name, 6
narrative, 6, 46, 65, 75, 76, 79, 93, 95, 97, 114, 123, 138, 140, 146, 158, 161
nature, 25, 54, 81, 128
necessity, 43
need, 57
negativity, 92
negotiation, 9
network, 15, 127
newfound, 12, 84
Nia, 149
niche, 101, 116, 152
night, 57, 94, 126, 127
nod, 6

Index 177

nomination, 62
norming, 67
nostalgia, 33, 48, 81, 84
note, 11, 53, 96, 111, 116, 127, 129

obscurity, 69
obstacle, 31
odyssey, 96
offer, 32
offering, 158
on, 1–3, 5–7, 12, 13, 16, 20, 23, 31, 33, 37, 39, 41–43, 45–47, 49, 51–53, 57, 61, 63, 64, 68, 70, 72, 73, 76, 78–83, 87, 93, 95–97, 100, 102–104, 107, 108, 111–114, 116–118, 120–122, 124, 126–130, 135, 141, 142, 144, 147, 151, 152, 155, 160–163
one, 2, 6, 9, 11, 25, 27, 32, 39, 43, 48, 57, 62, 69, 72, 76, 79, 80, 84, 91, 93, 97, 115, 129, 150
opportunity, 15, 20, 49, 81, 83, 146
other, 2, 7, 11, 12, 15, 16, 27, 33, 73, 77, 81, 87, 107, 141, 147, 150, 162–164
outage, 32, 48
outcome, 61
outlet, 147
output, 23, 67
overview, 135

palette, 22, 81
part, 37, 39, 49, 54, 69, 93, 102
participation, 20
partner, 57

partnership, 22, 23, 41, 43, 62, 63, 99, 142
passion, 1, 2, 4, 7, 10, 16, 37, 49, 71, 80, 82–84, 94, 96, 107, 112, 116, 128, 143, 145, 150, 159, 162, 163
past, 5, 81, 97, 116, 140
path, 2–4, 6, 15, 23, 33, 81, 95, 97, 100
pause, 82
people, 11, 12, 163
perception, 57, 75, 76, 116
performance, 3, 7, 15, 16, 32, 48, 49, 51, 53, 82, 96, 121, 139, 143
period, 3, 9, 10, 17, 39, 66, 71, 75–77, 80–85, 87, 93, 97, 146, 159
perseverance, 6, 16, 94, 99, 116, 145, 148, 163
persistence, 126
person, 92, 127
persona, 41, 77
perspective, 12, 22, 71, 94, 141
petition, 92
phase, 10, 12, 17, 27, 46, 64, 97
phenomenon, 48
philanthropic, 109, 122, 130, 160
philanthropy, 97, 104, 105, 107, 109, 117, 118
philosophy, 22
photography, 83
piece, 81
pioneer, 62
place, 37, 52, 59, 62, 66, 93, 94, 114, 140
platform, 47, 52, 97, 100, 105, 106, 117, 122, 139, 145, 152, 160

play, 7, 49, 113, 117, 129
playing, 12
plethora, 158
plunge, 14
point, 22, 43, 94
pop, 2, 3, 5, 9, 13, 14, 23, 26, 34, 62, 64, 94, 100, 101, 117, 123, 159
popularity, 12, 15, 21, 52, 152
portrayal, 76
position, 76, 110
possibility, 37
potential, 47, 56, 64, 78
power, 1, 2, 6, 12, 16, 21, 23, 32, 47, 48, 50, 64, 71, 73, 77, 84, 87, 92, 99, 109–111, 113, 116, 118, 124, 126, 129, 130, 143, 150, 160–163
powerhouse, 14
practice, 13, 16, 70, 79
precedent, 142
preparation, 3
presence, 15, 16, 28, 45–47, 113, 146
presentation, 15
press, 79
pressure, 1, 11, 13, 14, 27, 31, 42, 48, 53–55, 63, 76, 93, 96, 147
problem, 6
process, 2, 5, 9, 10, 19, 21, 22, 25–30, 42, 54, 61, 63, 65, 66, 68, 72–74, 79, 87, 94, 143, 151, 161, 163, 164
producer, 22, 28, 30, 62, 94, 151, 152
product, 63, 126
production, 22, 27, 34, 46, 72, 151
professional, 32, 70, 71, 135
program, 20, 83

progress, 4, 6, 32, 72, 162
progression, 25, 34
project, 62, 143
promise, 37
promoter, 151
prose, 162
prospect, 100
prowess, 138, 146, 153, 162
public, 6, 41, 55, 57, 75–77, 79, 92, 116, 159
publication, 163
pulse, 80
purpose, 2, 49, 81, 82, 84, 87, 97, 106
pursuit, 36, 71, 96

quality, 21, 32, 63, 84
quantity, 21
quest, 16, 36
question, 2, 85

Rachel Adams, 152
radio, 12, 22, 34
rate, 59
reach, 12, 22, 52, 109, 112, 113, 122, 164
reaction, 6
reading, 76
reality, 7, 76, 127
realization, 6, 51, 81
realm, 47, 54, 105, 114
rebirth, 89
recognition, 11, 12, 36, 37, 53, 64, 69, 96, 112, 114, 121, 122, 144, 146
record, 41, 92, 159
recording, 6, 13, 23, 27–31, 34, 53, 63, 68, 85, 94, 105
rediscovery, 81, 94

Index 179

reflection, 1, 67, 76, 84, 116, 120, 126
refuge, 1
regrouping, 84
rehearsal, 78
reinvention, 87, 94, 150
rejection, 1, 6
relatability, 161
relationship, 14, 31, 32, 51, 53, 57, 75–77, 91, 93, 103, 111, 118, 120, 127, 149
release, 35, 43, 92, 123, 140
relevance, 114, 150
reminder, 37, 49, 50, 59, 76, 86, 92, 117, 126, 130, 143, 145, 161
remix, 112
renewal, 91
repertoire, 2, 16
representation, 45
reputation, 12, 47, 141
research, 162, 163
resilience, 3, 7, 12, 14, 17, 22, 29, 37, 48, 59, 66, 69, 71, 87, 89, 91, 94–97, 114, 116, 143, 147, 148, 150, 152, 160, 163
resolve, 12, 27, 30, 37, 43, 93, 96, 127
resonance, 34, 52, 65, 122, 152, 161
respect, 62, 73, 96, 111, 163
response, 64, 76, 138
responsibility, 105, 118, 122, 160
rest, 83
result, 34, 36, 51, 55, 122
resurgence, 93
retreat, 81
retrospect, 33, 37
return, 81, 84, 87

reunion, 81
reverb, 34
rhythm, 10
ride, 127
riff, 34
rift, 57, 68, 76
right, 6, 34
rise, 22, 99, 112, 159
river, 72
road, 6, 11, 83, 97
rock, 2, 3, 9, 14, 22, 23, 26, 34, 64, 94, 100, 117, 123, 159
role, 3, 27, 30, 48, 56, 69, 73, 75, 79, 83, 92, 93, 97, 107, 112, 113, 117, 128, 151, 159, 161, 162
routine, 147
rumor, 79

s, 2, 3, 6, 10, 12–14, 21, 22, 25–28, 30, 31, 34, 37, 39, 43–48, 50–52, 54–56, 61–64, 66–69, 73, 75–79, 81, 87, 92–97, 99–105, 107, 109, 111, 112, 114–118, 120, 122, 123, 130, 135, 138–149, 151–153, 155, 157–161, 164
sabbatical, 83
saga, 76
Sam, 83, 147
Sam Patel's, 147
Samir, 149
sanctuary, 1, 27, 81
saturation, 21
scale, 112
scene, 3, 11, 12, 14–16, 118
scholarship, 146
school, 3, 146

scrutiny, 36, 55, 76, 78
section, 19, 25, 27, 30, 41, 43, 54, 61, 75, 77, 87, 91, 95, 101, 105, 118, 120, 127, 138, 141, 146, 152
selection, 162
self, 2, 4, 6, 10, 11, 26, 32, 39, 48, 49, 58, 70, 83, 84, 97, 99, 102, 147
sensation, 37
sensationalism, 76
sense, 2–4, 6, 11, 13, 15, 20, 21, 37, 48, 49, 58, 66, 78, 81, 82, 84, 87, 92, 99, 106, 109, 111, 114, 120, 127, 159, 161
series, 46, 49, 59, 61, 81, 93, 103, 141, 162
session, 13, 25, 32
set, 17, 23, 43, 47, 48, 83, 99, 123, 142, 146, 160, 161
setback, 3, 48, 71
setting, 10, 52
share, 2, 12, 20, 25, 30, 37, 51, 52, 62, 65, 66, 82, 92, 99, 106, 117, 127, 158, 161
shield, 2
shift, 64, 72, 159
shout, 127
show, 3, 6, 20, 37, 48, 49, 143
side, 76, 85, 87
sign, 6
significance, 43, 52, 61, 118, 150, 155, 157, 162
signing, 42
simplicity, 81
sing, 48, 153
singer, 151
single, 22, 43, 62, 112, 114

situation, 23, 57, 76, 78
size, 11
skepticism, 2
society, 107, 111, 122, 160
socio, 116, 158, 159
solace, 1, 66, 161
solidarity, 58, 76–80
solo, 80, 81, 85–87, 97, 147
solution, 73
song, 6, 10, 22, 23, 33, 34, 46, 51, 62, 63, 68, 73, 81, 100, 114, 116, 138, 139
songwriter, 62, 151
songwriting, 4, 22, 25–27, 81, 94, 99, 101, 102, 142, 147, 159, 163
Sophie Lin, 151
soul, 27, 62, 143
sound, 2–6, 9, 10, 12–15, 21, 22, 25–27, 31, 32, 34, 43, 45, 55, 56, 59, 61–63, 66, 68, 72, 73, 81, 83, 87, 93, 94, 96, 100, 101, 104, 112, 114, 116, 117, 128, 140–142, 146, 150, 152, 159, 160
soundscape, 34
soundtrack, 116, 127, 161
source, 69, 120
space, 27, 58, 70, 81
spark, 5, 96, 160
speaking, 114
specter, 93
speculation, 75–77, 79, 80, 92, 96
spelling, 6
spirit, 6, 23, 25, 59, 71, 82, 99, 115, 143, 148, 151, 155, 159, 163
split, 75

spotlight, 58, 59, 63, 76, 77, 82, 84, 117, 128
spring, 143
stability, 13
stadium, 123
stage, 2, 3, 10, 11, 15, 17, 43, 47, 48, 114, 127, 146, 163
stand, 11, 15, 128
standout, 138, 152
status, 12, 47, 57, 63
staying, 138, 160
step, 64, 71, 82, 84, 85
sticking, 72
sting, 1
stone, 33, 37
stop, 49
storm, 78, 80
storming, 67
story, 5, 30, 37, 43, 49, 59, 69, 76, 77, 87, 89, 93, 97, 118, 123, 126, 127, 130, 138, 140, 145, 150, 157, 160, 161, 164
storytelling, 21, 47, 63, 147, 162, 163
strain, 13, 72
straitjacket, 53
strategy, 20
streaming, 113, 153
strength, 2, 69, 120, 127
stress, 13, 53
strife, 91
structure, 34
struggle, 12, 14, 27, 36, 72, 94
studio, 14, 27, 28, 30, 84, 87, 94
study, 160
style, 3, 9, 15, 22, 23, 61–63, 72, 97, 100, 102, 112, 141, 153, 159

success, 7, 10, 13, 19, 21, 33, 34, 36, 43–45, 47, 51, 53, 54, 56, 69–72, 74, 82, 84, 93, 96, 100, 102, 110, 112, 114, 116, 120, 121, 123, 128, 143–145, 151, 152, 158
summary, 12, 23, 47, 66, 104, 122, 138, 155
summer, 6
support, 2, 31, 32, 36, 37, 52, 58, 76, 79, 80, 87, 91–93, 106, 117, 118, 120, 126, 127, 129, 139, 145, 149, 160, 164
surrounding, 77, 92, 158
sustainability, 160
sword, 36, 42, 77
Sydney, 114
symbol, 89
symphony, 99
synergy, 1, 25, 39, 62, 94, 96
synth, 55, 62

table, 5, 9, 23, 25, 93
take, 6, 52, 59, 79, 83, 122, 127, 160
tale, 116, 123, 146, 158
talent, 3, 6, 48, 59, 100, 117, 126, 128, 143, 146, 155, 163
tapestry, 2, 5, 7, 9, 22, 25, 27, 39, 93, 95, 97, 118, 123, 126, 127, 129, 141, 145
task, 14, 63, 161
taste, 37
team, 39, 52, 61, 76, 79, 128
teamwork, 3, 149
tear, 127
technology, 27, 66
term, 19, 57
terrain, 43

test, 77
testament, 6, 21, 23, 37, 45, 49, 50, 59, 62, 64, 66, 71, 84, 87, 89, 99, 102, 109, 111, 112, 116, 120, 122, 124, 126, 129, 135, 140, 142, 147, 150, 160, 161, 163
theater, 3
theme, 43, 161
theory, 4, 48, 57, 67
therapy, 147
thing, 97
thought, 7, 162
thread, 7, 127
thrill, 6, 39, 47–49
thrive, 159
ticket, 13, 31
time, 2, 23, 37, 52, 58, 83, 84, 87, 97, 116, 127, 159, 165
timeline, 42, 143
togetherness, 6
Tokyo, 114
toll, 70, 76, 82
tool, 10, 20, 46, 73, 116, 160, 162
tour, 37, 39, 49, 50, 57, 68, 93, 128, 144
touring, 31, 37, 39, 82, 85, 147
track, 6, 22, 23, 36, 62, 94, 100, 155
traction, 14
trajectory, 41, 43, 63, 67, 160
transformation, 42
transition, 42, 47
transparency, 21, 47, 66, 77
trend, 97
triumph, 61
trophy, 61
trust, 2, 21
truth, 76, 91, 110
Tuckman, 67

turmoil, 57
turning, 2, 22, 43, 94, 127
turnout, 11
twist, 62

uncertainty, 4, 6, 87, 93
understanding, 10, 16, 21, 27, 51, 54, 97, 111, 160
unit, 85
unity, 6, 22, 30, 47, 69, 77, 79, 116, 145
up, 1–4, 11, 62, 76, 100, 101, 117, 161
upheaval, 23
uplift, 109, 148
urge, 64
use, 21, 25, 34, 107, 109, 111, 114

validation, 6
validity, 78
value, 21
variable, 61
variety, 68, 141
venue, 6, 47, 48
verge, 78
versatility, 59, 141, 147, 162
viability, 2, 14, 31, 45, 55
vibe, 13
video, 46, 47, 93
view, 76
vinyl, 2
visibility, 12, 113, 139
vision, 13, 14, 27, 30, 54, 63, 68, 73, 79, 94, 97, 116, 142, 160, 163
visual, 15, 45, 47, 71
visualization, 48
vocal, 34, 62, 146, 147
vocalist, 51, 81, 143, 146

Index

voice, 14, 36, 78, 105, 109, 159, 163
voting, 121
voyage, 12
vulnerability, 5, 10, 58, 81, 99, 159, 161

wave, 117
way, 1, 20, 21, 66, 74, 114, 118, 126, 128, 143, 161
wealth, 87
weather, 80
weight, 20, 36, 37, 55, 60, 81, 94
well, 3, 32, 39, 52, 58, 83, 121, 147, 159
wellness, 39, 147
whirlwind, 36, 82, 85
whole, 107
willingness, 10, 23, 26, 27, 64, 73, 81, 83, 117, 123

win, 59
work, 6, 12, 23, 25, 30, 32, 59, 63, 64, 71, 87, 94, 109, 126, 146, 147, 158, 161–163
world, 2, 6, 22, 64, 66, 72, 74, 76, 77, 82, 97, 102, 109, 111, 114, 120, 122, 127, 147, 150, 161, 164
writer, 27
writing, 3, 63, 162

year, 59
yearning, 36
yoga, 84
youth, 1, 6

Zara K, 23
zeitgeist, 159